The End of Sex

ALSO BY DONNA FREITAS

Sex and the Soul

Killing the Imposter God

Becoming a Goddess of Inner Poise

The End of Sex

How Hookup Culture Is
Leaving a Generation Unhappy,
Sexually Unfulfilled, and
Confused About Intimacy

DONNA FREITAS

BASIC BOOKS
A Member of the Perseus Books Group
New York

Published by Basic Books,
A Member of the Perseus Books Group

Books published by Basic Books are available at special discounts for bulk purchases in the United States by corporations, institutions, and other organizations. For more information, please contact the Special Markets Department at the Perseus Books Group, 2300 Chestnut Street, Suite 200, Philadelphia, PA 19103, or call (800) 810-4145, ext. 5000, or e-mail special.markets@perseusbooks.com.

Book design by Cynthia Young

Library of Congress Cataloging-in-Publication Data
Freitas, Donna.
The end of sex : how hookup culture is leaving a generation unhappy,
    sexually unfulfilled, and confused about intimacy / Donna Freitas.
        pages cm
    ISBN 978-0-465-00215-3 (pbk. : alk. paper)—
    ISBN 978-0-465-03783-4 (e-book)   1. College students—Sexual behavior.
2. Youth—Sexual behavior.   3. Sexual ethics.   4. Dating (Social customs)
5. Intimacy (Psychology)   I. Title.

HQ27.F74 2013
176'.4—dc23

                                                2012042226

10 9 8 7 6 5 4 3 2 1

Contents

Author's Note

It was while teaching an undergraduate course at a small Catholic college that I first heard students talk extensively about hooking up.* Hookup culture was clearly dominant on campus, and my students were more than willing to discuss the sexual

---

*For anyone familiar with my book *Sex and the Soul: Juggling Sexuality, Spirituality, Romance and Religion on America's College Campuses*, published by Oxford University Press in 2008, the story that follows—about why I set out to interview college students about their sex lives and religious leanings—will sound familiar. Some of the data and student commentary I refer to in this book comes directly from *Sex and the Soul*—but for the purposes of taking a more focused and exclusive look at hookup culture. It was necessary for me to refer to those findings as well as subsequent, relevant data in order to introduce new readers to my study, open up new arguments about hookup culture, and ground my recommendations about how to respond to hookup culture.

encounters occurring at parties and in the residence halls on the weekends. At first no one complained about this culture—they accepted it as the norm and seemed perfectly happy living within it. Then, about halfway through the term, something changed. It took only one student to admit that hookup culture wasn't all she'd been told it was, and, what was more, that it made her miserable.* Suddenly, the students who had been speaking about hooking up in the most spirited of terms reversed themselves entirely. They confessed that they had been lying to one another about their real feelings.

This single day of confession changed the direction of student discussion for the remainder of the semester. From then on, my students explored what they felt was the real truth about sex and hooking up on campus. They started to question whether most people were satisfied with hookups as the norm, suspecting that their peers, if given the choice, would prefer to date and have long-term relationships. Their discussions revealed an intense longing for meaning—meaningful sex, meaningful relationships, and meaningful dates, and their corresponding classwork presented a devastating analysis of how and why hookup culture deprives students of the opportunity to fulfill their true desires and to experience sex that is good, while leaving

---

*For the full story about my class, please see the preface to Donna Freitas, *Sex and the Soul: Juggling Sexuality, Spirituality, Romance and Religion on America's College Campuses* (New York: Oxford University Press, 2008), xiii–xx.

many of them feeling isolated and lonely during their college experience.

The students became so passionate about the subject of what was missing from hookup culture that they created a newspaper to expand the conversation campus-wide. In it, they wrote of how they had learned to resist monogamous relationships in order to avoid being left out of hookup culture. As a consequence, they had become unable to "create valuable and real connections." They talked of "deserv[ing] more than 3 am–10 am, three nights a week," from a partner, and of their desire to "go on actual dates, and insist on commitment." They wondered what it would be like to stop tolerating the hookup as the norm. Was it possible, they wanted to know, to break the cycle of hookup culture and replace it with sex that was "healthier on an emotional, physical, and spiritual level," and even "meaningful, special, and sacred"?*

The class was something of a revelation to me, and I began to wonder if students at other universities felt the same way.† So I designed and launched a national study to find out. In the spring of 2006, I provided more than 2,500 college

---

*My class's one-issue newspaper was entitled *Dateline SMC*. These quotes came from two front-page articles, "Weekend Cinderellas" and "Is the Red Solo Cup Keeping Us Solo?"

†Although hookup culture is not exclusive to colleges, as it exists both before and after the university years, I chose to study institutions of higher education because of my many years of experience teaching on

students from all over the country with three private forums for discussing their spiritual and religious leanings (or non-leanings), and, in particular, how they felt about sex during college. I conducted an online survey; did in-depth, in-person interviews; and collected a series of journals that students wrote for the purposes of the study over a two-week period. The assembled data provided an extraordinarily rich picture of how students experience college today. Much like my own students, the subject they brought up over and over again was hookup culture.

Altogether, seven colleges and universities participated in this formal research on sex, romance, hookup culture, and dating on campus.* Diverse in terms of ranking, geography, economic status, and religious affiliation, these seven schools were chosen

---

college campuses as well as living and working on them for various departments of student affairs. The college campus provides a unique type of community in which young adults live on their own; it also provides a setting in which hookup culture thrives. Some students do not encounter hookup culture until they go to college. The vast majority of college freshmen are already acquainted with it from high school and even middle school, but the residential college campus is nevertheless where hookup culture intensifies for them. It begins to dominate their social lives and intimate relationships at a level previously unknown to their experience.

*Both the names of the participating institutions and the names of students have been kept anonymous to protect the privacy of everyone concerned. The assurance of privacy also allowed me to create conditions

for a number of additional reasons, including the willingness of the institutions to distribute the survey, their comfort with the study and their interest in allowing the research to be done on campus, and the strength of the relationships I had formed with my contacts on each campus. I focused on four different types of institutions: private-secular and public colleges (both of which I will call "secular," for the sake of brevity), evangelical colleges, and Catholic colleges. One of the findings of the study was that hookup culture was dominant—and essentially indistinguishable—at the participating secular and Catholic colleges. At evangelical colleges, however, hookup culture does not really exist. What you find instead is purity culture, an ostensibly

---

in which students could discuss the topic of sex on campus honestly and openly. The online survey sample was about two-thirds female and one-third male, and the interview sample was about 55 percent female and 45 percent male. Approximately 5 percent of the total population identified as gay, lesbian, or bisexual, and the students were distributed about evenly across each of the four college years. The vast majority of the students identified themselves as white/Caucasian (about 85 percent), most reported they were Christian (20 percent Roman Catholic, 32 percent evangelical Protestant, and 19 percent mainline Protestant), and they had come to college from 45 different states. Of the 2,500 students surveyed at the seven participating schools, 111 were randomly chosen from 534 volunteers to engage in extensive one-on-one, face-to-face interviews, all of whom I met in person and with whom I spoke on their respective campuses. Each of these students kept an online journal for a period of two weeks to chronicle their thoughts about the topics I was studying.

heterosexual culture that revolves around waiting to have sex—
or in some cases even a kiss—until marriage. The results of my
study were published in 2008 in *Sex and the Soul: Juggling Sexuality, Spirituality, Romance and Religion on America's College
Campuses*. That book chronicles my initial, general findings
about sex, hookup culture, religion, and spirituality on campus
(including extensive data from the participating evangelical
colleges).

In this book I both reiterate and refine some of those initial
findings, but more central than this, I focus in greater depth
on the data I gathered on hookup culture. Hookup culture is
a complicated phenomenon and I believe it deserves a book
of its own.* Many students resist defining their hookups with
specific, sexual content, so even a basic understanding of the
term "hookup" requires a certain amount of analysis. The gender and sexual identity politics of hookup culture are also complicated, as are the personal experiences of those who
participate in it.

My research into hookup culture has continued—and expanded—since the publication of *Sex and the Soul*. Over the

---

*Purity culture among evangelical youth is also complex and deserving
of extensive attention. Several recent books on the topic engage it at
length, including Christine J. Gardner's excellent *Making Chastity Sexy:
The Rhetoric of Evangelical Abstinence Campaigns*, which traces the politics and expanding popularity of purity pledges among youth.

course of my study I have learned about almost every aspect of this topic on college campuses today. Even more importantly, I have been afforded an extensive, inside look at hookup culture that few can claim, including fellow researchers and journalists who have written on the topic. Professors have taught *Sex and the Soul* across disciplines from education and sociology to psychology and religious studies, with some developing entire courses around the subjects I covered. Higher education professionals working in student affairs departments have used the book for professional development and to justify new programming on their campuses, and offices of campus ministry have devoted retreats to discussing how my findings might affect their work with students. I have lectured at dozens of educational institutions across the United States, from small colleges to huge universities, in rural America and in major cities. These lectures have given me the opportunity to informally continue the conversation on sex and hookup culture with thousands more students as well as concerned faculty, staff, and university administrators and their colleagues.

Taken together, these experiences have deepened my understanding of how students manage to find meaning (or not) within hookup culture. I have learned from these visits that hookup culture continues unabated, and that many, many students struggle in silence with their lack of options for sexual and romantic intimacy. These experiences have solidified for me not only what is at stake for students during their university experience, but also what is missing from their discussions both inside and outside of the lecture halls.

One of the things I have learned from the reaction to *Sex and the Soul*, however, is that hookup culture is not inevitable. Parents, professors, university administrators, and the students themselves are capable of finding—even driven to find—meaningful alternatives. Over the past few years I have been lucky enough to witness the incredible effort that higher education personnel are making to respond to the needs of the students in their care. I have met professors who are deeply concerned about their students beyond the classroom, and I have been amazed by the dedication and creativity they bring to the task of navigating the waters of this culture in which their students are immersed.

I hope this book will help to keep the conversation around hookup culture moving forward. But more importantly, I hope that my suggestions for dealing with hookup culture will enable educators, parents, and students alike to respond productively to a problem that can sometimes seem monolithic. Over the course of nearly twenty years of teaching, I have never seen young women and men struggle with any other issue the way they are struggling with hookup culture. I care deeply about those living, breathing bodies sitting in front of me in the classroom, and feel a responsibility to take action as best as I can. I am not interested in legislating over their lives, but in finding

the various frameworks necessary to promote their empowerment from within. My greatest wish is to help make available
a set of diverse structures through which students can make
the best, most informed choices they can about their bodies
and their lives.

Introduction

The Second Shift of College

AMID THE SEEMINGLY ENDLESS PARTYING on America's college campuses lies a thick layer of melancholy, insecurity, and isolation that no one can seem to shake. College students have perfected an air of bravado about hookup culture, though a great many of them privately wish for a world of romance and dating. And yet they soldier on. By all appearances, graduating college with sex on one's social resumé is as important as it is to have a range of activities, internship experiences, and a solid GPA on the professional one. In today's college culture, sex is something students fit into their schedules, like studying and going to the gym.

College students learn from the media, their friends, and even their parents that it's not sensible to have long-term relationships in college. College is a special time in life—they will never get the chance to learn so much, meet so many people, or have as much fun again. Relationships restrict freedom—they require more care, upkeep, and time than anyone can afford to give during this exciting period between adolescence and adulthood. They add pressure to the already heavily pressured, overscheduled lives of today's students, who, according to this ethos, should be focusing on their classes, their job prospects, and the opportunity to party as wildly as they can manage. Hookups allow students to get sex onto the college CV without adding any additional burdens, ensuring that they don't miss out on the all-American, crazy college experience they feel they must have. They can always settle down later.

Students play their parts—the sex-crazed frat boy, the promiscuous, lusty coed—and they play them well. But all too often they enact these highly gendered roles for one another because they have been taught to believe that hookup culture is normal, that everyone is enjoying it, and that there is something wrong with them if they don't enjoy it, too. What could be better than sex without strings? Yet, in fact, many of them—both men and women—are not enjoying it at all.

Hookup sex is fast, uncaring, unthinking, and perfunctory. Hookup culture promotes bad sex, boring sex, drunken sex you don't remember, sex you could care less about, sex where desire is absent, sex that you have "just because everyone else is, too," or that "just happens." It's the new, second shift of college: the housework, the domestic labor that everyone needs to pitch in and get through because it simply has to get done. The more students talk about hooking up, the clearer it becomes that it has less to do with excitement or even attraction than with checking a box off a long list of tasks, like homework or laundry. And while hookup sex is supposed to come with no strings attached, it nonetheless creates an enormous amount of stress and drama among participants.

Today's younger generation learns quickly and learns well that the norm is to be casual about sex—even though so many of them don't fit this "norm." Parents and educational institutions unwittingly promote this idea. Because we worry about the perils of casual sex among teens—unwanted pregnancy, sexually transmitted infections (STIs), and, for some constituencies, sin and God's disapproval—the very people who should be mentoring young men and women about the pleasures and joys of good sex instead focus on its dangers. Sex education in high schools, in both its comprehensive and abstinence-only forms, tends to favor the how-to's or the why-not-to's of sex. This limited approach is often reiterated in first-year college orientations, which tend to concentrate on birth control, STIs, and sexual assault. Rather than empowering teens and young adults to make informed decisions about sex, these sex-educational methods often reinforce the idea that hookup culture is the norm, that everyone is doing it, and that all students can do is protect themselves against its worst excesses.

The average college student, like the average adult, wants to have a meaningful sex life, even a soulful one, even if that requires having less sex or, for a time, no sex. But the path toward this goal is dimly lit. This leaves students fumbling all the way up to their senior year, sensing that something is missing from their lives, yet with no idea how to find fulfillment or who can help them in their search for it. Universities may be doing a good enough job facilitating safe sex for those who genuinely enjoy hooking up. But many students today are graduating college either unhappy or ambivalent about their sex lives, and unable to imagine a more fulfilling alternative. At the center of their unease is the four years they've lived within hookup culture.

BUT WHERE DID HOOKUP CULTURE come from? I've been asked this again and again during the question-and-answer sessions at my lectures. As yet, there are no true historians of hookup culture who can trace the exact evolution of the practice and back up their claims with data.[1] We do, however, have a number of snapshots of hookup culture during particular years or months. Some have been provided by journalists who have gathered anecdotal information, such as Laura Sessions Stepp, who in 2007 wrote the first book-length treatment of the subject, entitled *Unhooked: How Young Women Pursue Sex, Delay Love, and Lose at Both*, which focused on women's experience. In *Hooking Up: Sex, Dating, and Relationships on Campus*, a more academic work than Stepp's, Kathleen Bogle offered a history of hookup culture. She did not, however, provide a satisfactory answer to how it arose and how it gained so much ground, before moving on to discuss the results of her study on hooking up at college. Bogle's history of dating begins with the "calling era," moves on to the more traditional date and "going steady," and has the hookup emerging amorphously out of changes wrought by the women's movement and the sexual revolution.[2]

Hookups have existed throughout human history, of course, but what is now happening on American campuses is something different. College has gone from being a place where hookups happened to a place where hookup culture dominates student attitudes about all forms of intimacy. The hookup has become *normative*, and hookup culture a monolithic culture from which students find little chance of escape. It is the defining aspect of social life on many campuses; to reject it is to relegate oneself to the sidelines of college experience.

In my personal experience as a university student in the early to mid-1990s, the hookup was one of many available forms of relating. Hookup culture was like a town everyone knew about and knew how to find. We also knew who lived there permanently and partied there exclusively. Most of us would visit hookup culture and its accompanying parties a number of times during college, if only to see what it was like. But we weren't immersed in it throughout our four years—or, at least, we didn't have to be if we didn't want to. The landscape for navigating one's romantic and sexual life was much broader and more diverse and included traditional dates and long-term romantic relationships as well as hooking up. (There was also the possibility of opting out of all of it.) But even in the mid-1990s, hooking up could still mean making out at a party and exchanging phone numbers, with the thought of turning the make-out session into an opportunity for a relationship. It didn't necessarily ride on the notion of unattached intimacy both during and afterward, and it wasn't an end in itself.

Between 1997 and 2003, I lived on campus as a professional in student affairs departments at two major universities, one Catholic and one private-secular. More than anything else, student alcohol abuse was the major issue. My colleagues and I dealt with it on a regular basis with the students in our residence halls. Hookup culture existed then, too, but it didn't dominate the social lives of students the way it does now. I witnessed couples heading out on dates, knew of long-term relationships that were kindled early on in a student's first year of college, and listened as students chatted about their various social exploits and romantic aspirations. It wasn't until my last few years living in the halls that student behavior became more extreme, and the drunken hookups more obvious because they began in the hallways, stairwells, and elevators in my building. But still, among the students with whom I came into contact for all sorts of student-affairs department reasons, conversation about hooking up was fairly minimal. You might hear the term once in a while, but it was not the thing that everyone was talking about constantly. Today, it's almost the only thing.

One can only speculate as to the reasons that hookup culture has come to dominate college campuses in the early part of the twenty-first century. During the 1980s and 1990s, the threat of AIDS loomed over all sexual encounters. Today's generation has a difficult time understanding the threat of AIDS, given advances in research and medication. The widespread availability and social acceptance of pornography is yet another factor that may contribute to the rise of hookup culture over the past decade. The ubiquitousness of pornography is changing the attitudes of young adults about sex, their expectations for their partners, and their understanding of desire, gender identity, and how one enters into various types of sexual intimacy.

Moreover, the campus culture—along with the wider culture—has become more superficial with the advance of technology. A frenetic *go-go-go* and *do-do-do* pace, increasing in the midst of an economic recession, has put young adults under ever more pressure. They are competing with each other for fewer and fewer jobs, but burdened with greater and greater expectations of success. Such pressure can breed stress, anxiety, and even selfishness, all of which are aided and abetted by technologies that allow us to text rather than call, and to interact superficially and efficiently, with broad swaths of "friends" and followers, through Facebook and Twitter, rather than engage in meaningful interactions face to face with other human beings. This pace and pressure coincide with the attitudes toward others fostered by hookup culture. Rather than looking at the people right in front of us, we look at our phones, preferring to touch a screen rather than the hand of a partner. Instead of engaging in conversation with those sitting next to us, we text, email, and chat with people nowhere near our bodies. We have become more excited about interacting with the various technological devices at our disposal than about developing relationships with real people, even our own children. This prioritizing of technology over in-person interactions does not teach us how to value the life and body of another human being, or what it means to treat others with dignity and respect. Instead, it promotes the idea that in-person relationships are cumbersome and time consuming—better to be dealt with online, or, even better, not at all.[3]

ONE OF THE MOST RECENT contributions to the cultural conversation about hookup culture comes from journalist Hanna Rosin, who, in her book *The End of Men*, argued, among other things, that the perfunctory nature of sex during a hookup is essential to support a wider landscape of sexual liberation and empowerment among today's young women. Ambivalent sex is useful, Rosin said, because it does not tie a young woman down—it allows her to focus exclusively on professional aspirations. "To put it crudely," she wrote, "feminist progress right now largely depends on the existence of the hookup culture. And to a surprising degree, it is women—not men—who are perpetuating the culture, especially in school, cannily manipulating it to make space for their success, always keeping their own ends in mind. For college girls these days, an overly serious suitor fills the same role an accidental pregnancy did in the 19th century: a danger to be avoided at all costs, lest it get in the way of a promising future."[4]

Rosin's argument is fascinating, but, based on my research, I believe it is also misleading. It is true that the existence of hookup culture allows young women to put off relationships.

Yet it doesn't simply *allow* this, it fairly *forbids* the formation of long-term romantic attachments, something both genders complain about in private. It is also true that women perpetuate the culture (just as men do), but many young women say they feel they have no other option. The same students who talk approvingly about hookup culture in certain settings (say, at a party, or in front of their friends in the dorms) will often denounce it in anonymous surveys or private personal interviews. Rosin's anecdotes about how young women feel about hookup culture were amassed in public, most while the women were drinking at a party. The difference between young adults' public and private personas tends to be vast, and it is a mistake to rely only on data gathered in public, especially with respect to hookup culture—a subject about which both women and men feel enormous social pressure.

Rosin's thesis is based on a broader—and even more troubling—assumption as well: that the vast majority of the young men available to women are really undatable boy-men—immature, embarrassing, pathetic, vulgar, sex-crazed "douchebags" as she puts it—people whom no self-respecting young woman would want around for longer than one night or even a few hours. Hookup culture is the only viable option in such a bleak landscape. Today's women are proudly sexual creatures, and they simply need to use men to scratch that itch. Women are not as "vulnerable" to heartbreak as they once were, in Rosin's opinion, and are so inured to men's vulgarity that she "found barely anyone who even *noticed* the vulgarity anymore." Rosin's analysis ultimately amounts to a plea on hookup culture's behalf, but it is a sad plea. Rather than expressing women's sexual liberation, hookup culture, according to Rosin, is based on a fundamental contempt for men. It is little more than a reversal of traditional roles—now women can treat men as badly as women have been treated over the centuries. It buys into the idea that vulnerability itself is a problem, celebrating steeliness and the ability to harden oneself against compassion and empathy. Is this really the great triumph of feminism? Seemingly so, according to Rosin. Anyone who argues against hookup culture, she suggested, is conservative, antifeminist, and anti–sexual revolution. Anyone who argues for a resurgence of dating and romance is merely nostalgic (as with Caitlin Flanagan's *Girl Land*).

Yet, how can we not question a culture that doesn't value relationships at all? If in the past women have been used as objects for the sexual gratification of men, does this mean that women's triumph lies in payback of the same? Or do true gains lie somewhere else in the landscape of sexuality and all that surrounds it?

THE CULTURAL CONVERSATION surrounding hookup culture should be about what we want our young people to get out of sex. It should offer a wide range of models for good sex and romantic relationship, with hooking up as one option among many. Conservative critics get it wrong when they judge young people for making sexual choices of which they disapprove—

young men and women should be free to make whatever choices suit them. But liberals get it wrong when they celebrate hookup culture as an antidote to patriarchy, as a utopia of human sexual liberation. The reality is that more and more young women and men are ambivalent, at best, about their sexual encounters. This brave new world is making very few people—men or women, gay or straight—happy.

I want young men and women of all sexual orientations to have great sex—if having sex is what they want. I want young adults to feel empowered, not cornered, about their sexual decision-making, to look forward to the promise of sexual intimacy, and to look back on their experiences with excitement and pride. Whether these feelings occur in a short-term relationship (even as short as a few hours) or a longer one is not the issue. Over the course of a lifetime, a person will experience many different types of sex, not all of them pleasurable, so to expect that every moment of sexual intimacy will be great, or even good, is unrealistic—this I understand. But to at least strive for good sex is not an unreasonable goal.

Hookup culture teaches young people that to become sexually intimate means to become emotionally empty, that in gearing themselves up for sex, they must at the same time drain themselves of feeling. They are acculturated to believe that they are *supposed* to regard sex as a casual, no-big-deal type of experience, yet many of them discover that sex is in fact a big deal. When I gave students the space to reflect privately on the attitudes they suspected their peers held about sex, 45 percent of student respondents at Catholic colleges and 36 percent at secular schools said that they personally did not feel casual about sex, but believed everyone else around them did. Many of these same students said they believed they *should* feel more casual so they could be more like their peers; some added that they wished their peers would be less casual about sex. Almost all the students who spoke about their peers' attitudes about sex said that the norm on campus was to be casual—period.[5]

Some students, about 23 percent, said they generally didn't care about the hookups they had. Hooking up was just "whatever," or it's just part of the deal when you go to college, an experience they could take or leave. The respondents who talked the most openly about sexual encounters were the students who also sounded like they were discussing household chores, and who made hookup culture sound like getting through a required class. Desire, if it was a part of the equation at all, seemed to play only a negligible role. Their reports about sexual intimacy seemed almost robotic.

Yet, most common of all among the respondents were the 41 percent of students who expressed sadness and even despair about hooking up. These students suspected that it robbed them of healthy, fulfilling sex lives; positive dating experiences; and loving relationships. At its very worst, hooking up made students feel "miserable" and "abused," and some students claimed that all it took was a hookup gone wrong and your college experience could be ruined—that one night could make or break your life at college for good.[6]

In the time since I conducted my initial survey, that middle group—the "whateverists"—seems to have become larger. Based on my ongoing visits to college campuses and conversations with undergraduates, I have come to believe that students are becoming more callous about sex—and perhaps about other things as well. This callousness does not read to me as liberation, but rather as defeat in the face of hookup culture's dominance. Young women and men have no other choice but to hook up, in their view, so they may as well do whatever is required to join in while minimizing the negative results. The rise and "progress" of hookup culture rests in the fact that young adults are simply getting better at being uncaring. But is being uncaring a skill we want young people to learn?

Sex—indeed, human relationships in general—should not be about treating others as a means to an end. Sex may sometimes, for some people, be an end in itself—but it should not be only this. We should be opening up young adults to a broad conversation about the many possible goods of sex and empowering them to ask about its meaning—and we should not only be doing so in the traditional settings of the sex-education class or the first-year orientation sex talk. We should be availing ourselves of an expansive set of resources toward this end, drawing on a variety of texts from the humanities and sciences. The university—the place where hookup culture dominates—is also the place best suited to opening up this dialogue. Rigorous, wide-ranging resources already exist on syllabi across the disciplines. All that professors and university personnel need to do is open up discussion to include questions about the meaning of sex.

Ideally, the college experience helps young adults learn how to navigate adult responsibilities and become the kind of self-aware, intelligent, tolerant citizens that university mission statements boast their campuses turn out into the world. Harvard University claims that its mission is to teach its students "productive cooperation"; they will learn "to assume responsibility for the consequences of personal actions," and the "collegiality [the university] fosters . . . will lead [students] in their later lives to . . . promote understanding, and to serve society." Yale aims to prepare its students "to contribute to the health and development of the human community." At the University of California at Los Angeles, the desire is to address "pressing societal needs and create a university enriched by diverse perspectives in which all individuals can flourish," as well as to "pass on to students a renewable set of skills and commitment to social engagement." The University of Notre Dame wants to promote "a disciplined sensibility to the poverty, injustice and oppression that burden the lives of so many" and to create "a sense of human solidarity and concern for the common good that will bear fruit as learning becomes service to justice." And at the University of Texas, the objective is "to cultivate in students the ethical and moral values that are the basis of a humane social order." These are just a few of the lofty declarations about the nature of the college experience today and the values that universities hope to cultivate.

Colleges and universities devote a good deal of time to educating students about human rights around the world, dignity, justice, social engagement, and the need to contribute to the betterment of the human community. Yet, when a hookup is not merely one possible forum for sexual intimacy among many but the expected norm for all, students learn to treat others as objects existing for the sole purpose of providing them a certain good, to be disposed of or put aside once they are done. Within a dominant culture of hooking up, it is normal—typical even—to use others as if they were without feelings or real value. The sheer amount of repression and suppression of emotion required for living in the context of hookup culture teaches young adults (or tries to teach them) not to feel at all.

We cannot encourage our students and children to become whole, integrated, empowered, virtuous people if we fail to adequately address hookup culture and to articulate how it works against these goals. In pretending that what happens after dark on campus doesn't matter, we are failing these young people and fooling ourselves about our roles as educators and parents. Whether the young adults coming onto our campuses want to hook up or not, they will be faced with hookup culture the moment they walk through the campus gates.

Understanding hookup culture is at the heart of the conversation about who we want our young people to grow up to be. Our intimate lives are not walled off from the rest of our lives, from our values and activities, our professional aspirations, and our personal conduct. If we live in a culture that teaches young people to care less about their own feelings, and everyone else's, that bodies are to be used and disposed of afterward, we can be sure that those lessons are going to spill over into everything else they do, and everything they are.

We need to talk to students about hookup culture, help them explore their feelings about it, and give them a chance to work through what they have learned about themselves from living within it. We need to consider the realities of hookup culture in the broader conversation about what it means to be responsible to oneself and to others, and what it means both to be an individual and part of a community. Ultimately, we need to empower them to seek the kinds of relationships they want, expanding their choices beyond that of simply succumbing to the hookup as their only option. But before we do any of this, we first have to listen to what young men and women have to say about this culture that greets them on their very first day of their college experience.

Hookup World:
The What, the Why, the How,
the Classic vs. the Serial

*Hooking up, I would say, is anything involving
kissing, touching, feeling, or any kind of sexual activity. It could be as small as kissing someone for a
few minutes, or as much as having sex with them.*

—JUNIOR MAN AT A PRIVATE-SECULAR UNIVERSITY

That's not okay, like, in Hookup World.

—JUNIOR WOMAN AT A PUBLIC UNIVERSITY

*There are no strings. You just do it, you're done,
and you can forget about it.*

—FIRST-YEAR WOMAN AT A CATHOLIC COLLEGE

CLEARLY, A "HOOKUP" TODAY is not about getting together
to go to the movies. But it isn't necessarily a one-night stand,
either. So many of us make assumptions about the term "hooking up" because we have heard it batted around on television,

read about it in newspapers and magazines, or overheard our children discussing it. We rarely stop our hand-wringing long enough to define our terms. What is a "hookup"? How does a sexual encounter qualify as one, and what makes it different from those that would not be considered in the same light?

Several articles that drew national attention gave the American public its first glimpses into hookup culture. In 2006, Caitlin Flanagan's much-talked-about article on the topic in *The Atlantic*, "Are You There God? It's Me, Monica," set off alarm bells far and wide. Flanagan wrote about an alleged blow-job epidemic among teenagers and puzzled over why, given the so-called female empowerment we had achieved, girls had become so careless about their own behavior and pleasure and so focused on pleasing boys sexually.[1] Then, in 2010, Flanagan took on hookup culture more directly with "Love, Actually," an article, also appearing in *The Atlantic*, about how hookup culture was robbing girls of the "Boyfriend Story" they really wanted. She wondered how sexual liberation had come to be equated with the ability to endure a hookup. Her own understanding of sexual liberation was something far more moderate and involved finding a middle road between sex equaling marriage, family, and domesticity, on the one hand, and sex equaling nothing at all, not even self-respect, on the other. Hookup culture not only robbed girls of the love story they really wanted, she said, it also robbed them of true sexual liberation.

Flanagan's critique was spot on, yet she fell into the trap of assuming, like so many people, that hookup culture was a

culture that served and was perpetuated by boys. This view leaves out a discussion of how boys feel about hookup culture. Also, like Hanna Rosin, who used anecdotal evidence to draw her conclusions, Flanagan failed to base her observations on rigorous data. Instead, she relied on personal reflection and news reports as "evidence" of what was going on with America's teens and young adults.

In order to understand hookup culture, it is important to move past such alarmist public dialogue in order to grasp what such an encounter is, according to young adults who actually engage in the behavior. The only definitions that matter are those given to us by the kids who are hooking up. To find out what those definitions are, we must ask them.

"HOOKING UP CAN VARY from a make-out session to having sex. . . . Then, with certain situations, you'll know that it's going to go further than that," said one young woman I interviewed, a sophomore at a Catholic college. By "further," she didn't mean physically, but emotionally. During a hookup, if a person allows emotions to enter into the experience, he or she is betraying the social contract a hookup requires and will have to pay for this transgression. "*That* is where you set yourself up for heartache," she said. "*That* is where that whole morning-after thing hurts."[2]

Another young woman, also a sophomore at a Catholic college, reiterated this belief. A hookup, as far as sexual intimacy goes, she said, is broadly understood to include just about every

type of activity imaginable. "A good number of people understand hooking up as a Saturday night they made out with someone. And that was that," she said. "Then there are people who
understand it as a Saturday night they had sex with someone.
And that was that. . . . There's no relationship, no strings attached. It's not supposed to be something that either person
dwells on. It's not supposed to go anywhere." For this young
woman and for most of the students with whom I have spoken,
the "anywhere" to which they are not supposed to go is a relationship, and the "something" on which they are not supposed to dwell is the sexual intimacy exchanged. Theoretically,
everyone is supposed to be able to walk away from the experience as if it did not happen, because this is what the social
contract asks of them.

The types of activities that hookups involve may leave out
emotional attachment, but they leave out little in the way of
what is permitted by the activity itself. On a number of occasions, students claimed that oral sex and kissing basically stood
side by side in the spectrum of sexual intimacy. A junior at a
private-secular university explained to me that oral sex has
"turned into the new making out." "Instead of just kissing,"
she said, "do that."

Nor is hooking up a phenomenon just for the straight man
or woman on campus. Gay and lesbian students are also caught
up in hookup culture. One woman, a senior at a secular university who identified as queer, said that although she equated
hooking up with kissing, she felt that for her friends and peers,

"oral sex is maybe [the] most preferred" type of sexual content. A gay sophomore at a Catholic school said that for his peers, a hookup could be anything from one-time sex during a "one-night stand" to occasional sex, "depending on your definition of sex." What defined a hookup more than the sex itself was the perception of its meaning (or lack thereof) by both participating parties. "It's nothing serious, and not expected to last," this sophomore stressed.

Other students had succinct descriptions of the hookup that were similar. A hookup is "one sexual encounter that has no commitment involved," said a first-year man at a Catholic college. "It's like you conquered something," said a junior at a private-secular school. The object of conquest for this young man was not so much a woman but fulfillment of a social expectation. This is true for many young men, who both engage in the behavior and are often its primary instigators.

A senior woman at a private-secular institution told me that a hookup was "purely physical [and] emotionally unattached." Another, at a private-secular university, said that a hookup "can run the gamut of any sexual activity . . . making out all the way to having sex." And a sophomore man at a public university echoed this refrain, describing a hookup as "any sort of romantic or sexual moment between any two people." He added, after a pause, that, "for some people, it's just a sexual conquest."

As for what people are supposed to get out of a hookup, the students were not always so certain: "sexual gratification," said one young man from a private-secular school, although he later added that he wasn't sure this was always, or even usually, the case, especially for the female parties involved.

THE ASSUMPTION BEHIND much of the alarm across the country about hookup culture has to do, in part, with the apparent acceptance of hookups as a fact of life among American youth. A corollary to this assumption is that reputations are no longer tarnished by sexual promiscuity, that something fundamentally different is happening on campus, because young people are blatant and matter of fact about their sexual interactions. But, as I found when talking in depth with some of the students I interviewed, this perception is not quite accurate.

I spoke with one young woman at a secular university—let's call her Sara—who covered just about every aspect of hookup culture in our conversation, from what it is, to who does it and why, to how it affects men as opposed to women. "I think of a hookup as a one-night stand kind of ordeal," said Sara, a junior. As college students tend to see hookups and one-night stands in different, though related categories, Sara's use of the phrase "kind of" expressed the fact that a hookup is something *like* a one-night stand, but not exactly a one-night stand. "[A hookup might happen] maybe one or two extra times," she said, "but pretty much . . . you don't even know this person and you're never going to see them again, or hope that you don't see them again. This is just about sex."

This understanding of the hookup is fairly universal among college students. But so is the concession that, by definition, the hookup doesn't usually work out this way. There often are strings, at least for one of the parties, and this creates drama and complications. "The problem is," Sara went on, "when one person goes into it [saying], 'Okay this is a hookup,' but it turns out one person always get attached. Unfortunately, most of the time, it's the girl." When I asked her to tell me more, she remarked: "That's not okay, like, in Hookup World. The thing about a hookup is, whoever shows remorse, or tries to turn it into a relationship, [is] the one that gets viewed badly." Reiterating that the person most likely to break this part of the social contract was the girl, she said, "I have female friends that have hooked up with a guy, and we all say she shouldn't have done that. But nothing really is [said] about the guy. . . . It [affects] how you view the hook up—who gets hurt."

Sara had a lot to say about how gender and the frequency of a person's hookups affect reputation. "The people that do hook up, hook up a lot," she said. "Some girls do have hookups, but then it's kind of a mistake and they don't do it again. Then there are other girls that you know sleep around a lot and it's frowned upon. Every time they say, 'He isn't calling me back,' most of the other girls are like, 'Well, I wonder why? You just slept with him, and you do that a lot.' Don't you think you would learn you should probably save yourself?"

In other words, despite the popular notion that hookup culture is rampant on campus, and that students engage in it without qualms, women are often harsh in their judgment of other women who hook up. Just about all of them are trying to play the game in a way that doesn't result in a tarnished reputation. "People talk, and people know what's going on," Sara said. "Typically, if a girl sleeps around a lot, a lot of the other girls will shun her or make comments to her about it. It's like the gender regulating her." According to Sara, the way "the gender regulates" women is through gossip. The "gender regulations" within hookup culture are set up to blame the woman if she gets into trouble. Women are supposed to go into hookup culture knowing the deal—that the male gender can get away with more hookups than the female gender—yet they go ahead and cross the line anyway. The subsequent gossip and low opinion of a woman who hooks up a lot—and whose hookups become public—is how she is "regulated" by the culture.

Men can also get into trouble, according to Sara—sort of. "If a girl were to come up to me and say, 'Don't talk to him, that guy's a slut,' I won't [do it]," Sara explained. Although guys with bad reputations "do find girls to sleep with," she reported, "if a guy has a bad reputation, then his chances of dating or talking to a girl who has a good reputation is very slim. He can sleep around if he wants, but it does come back in the end."

LIFE, IT SEEMS, IS MESSY, and hookups rarely fit into neat definitions. Looking at the hookup as a category gets complicated when viewed in light of a student's larger story of the experience. Yet, like Sara, most of the college students I spoke with at Catholic and secular institutions had detailed opinions about what counted as a hookup and how they believed their peers viewed hooking up, so it is possible to construct a basic definition. Typically, students used three major criteria to characterize the hookup:

1. A hookup includes some form of sexual intimacy, anything from kissing to oral, vaginal, or anal sex and everything in between.

2. A hookup is brief—it can last as short as a few minutes to as long as several hours over a single night.

3. A hookup is intended to be purely physical in nature and involves both parties shutting down any communication or connection that might lead to emotional attachment.

To sum up briefly, the three qualities that make up a hookup are its sexual content, its brevity, and its apparent lack of emotional involvement. Given the broad scope of sexual intimacy within a hookup, focusing on the first criterion, the sexual activity itself, for example, would lead us in the wrong direction, particularly if our intention was to help students tackle the angst, sadness, and frustration they felt about hookup culture. In my study, 77 percent of the student participants answered yes to a survey question that asked whether they had ever had oral, anal, or vaginal sex.[3] People love to focus on such findings—how many students, how many teens, how many unmarried young adults are having heterosexual sexual intercourse, what percentage are engaging in oral sex, and so on. We bat around such figures as if all heterosexual intercourse counts as hookup sex (it doesn't), and as if such numbers will give us solid data about hookup culture itself (they won't).[4]

Tackling hookup culture is far more complicated than this sort of statistic can convey. Raw data about sexual activity does not tell us what is most significant, because it does not tell us anything about the *quality* of the student's experience, how students *feel* about hookups after the fact, or what happens when a student's attempt at emotionally devoid sexual intimacy fails. It is impossible to draw accurate conclusions about hookup culture based on general data about sexual activity alone. If we never went further than the surface data, the real conversation that we could, and should, have about hookup culture would never occur. What makes a hookup a hookup is *not* the sexual content itself, per se (exactly what happened). The sexual content is but only part of the full story.[5]

More important is how a *student* decides to label an experience of sexual intimacy, regardless of what sort of sexual activity occurred. Also significant is the *conflict* that can arise between various students' interpretations of an intimate encounter and whether it is a hookup. One partner might label an experience a hookup, while the other hopes that it is the beginning of a relationship. Other students—those who witnessed the encounter or are aware of the encounter—may label the experience a hookup even if they know little about what actually happened or how the participants viewed it. This is true even if the experience involved only kissing. The category of "hookup" holds a certain amount of cachet within the campus peer group—sometimes as valuable gossip, sometimes as personal achievement, or as a reason to boast, or even as a label to avoid at all costs. Therefore, labeling something (or not) as a hookup can change a student's social status. In some cases, it will elevate that status, especially in the case of men who want to rack up "conquests." But it can just as easily hurt a person's social status, especially if that person is a woman. This is one of the major reasons why an outsider's interest in the specific nature of sexual content is less important than the label that *students* put on the encounter. The sexual content may even be beside the point. That any student (or students) would claim or disclaim an encounter involving sexual intimacy as a hookup is a much more significant factor.

Many college students in fact say that, in talking with others about their own hookups, they leave the sexual content of the hookup purposely vague, so that there is a mysterious quality attached to the recounting. If a student claims a hookup, then their peers automatically know that something happened, but no one really knows exactly what, unless that person is willing to give specifics. By withholding details, the student doing the telling is able to retain (or at least try to retain) some power.

For a woman, no matter what happened in a hookup, keeping the sexual content of the hookup vague keeps open the possibility that it might have just been a kiss. Downplaying the level of sexual intimacy in this way can help to protect her reputation, while still allowing her to claim that she hooked up. The opposite is true for men. For them, no matter what happened in the hookup, withholding details keeps open the possibility that something more happened than actually did.

The second criterion defining the hookup—its brevity—can also be misleading, if only because it does not tell the full story. The "classic hookup," as I've come to call it, is an encounter that doesn't last for more than a few hours during a single evening. To call it a one-night stand would be misleading, in part because students themselves do not tend to use this terminology. In many cases, such a description would also give the encounter too much weight. Claiming something as a one-night stand implies that one party sleeps over at the other's residence and that there is some sort of morning interaction. While some hookups may last an entire night, many do not. Staying together a full night into the morning could lead to unwanted drama, that dreaded walk of shame, or just too much involvement—involvement that, like emotional attachment, is to be avoided. In many cases, the shorter the hookup, the better. To hook up, many students will retire to an empty bedroom at a party for a bit, or even steal some time in an unoccupied bathroom. In cases where a hookup doesn't go much further than a make-out session, sometimes students will hook up in plain view of everyone they know—in a dark corner, on the couch, in the middle of the dance floor—which is all the better for the exchanges of gossip that will occur the next day.

Brief and uncomplicated at least in its intention, the hookup is a sexual encounter a student can "get done" in a short period of time, even as little as fifteen minutes. A hookup (at least in theory) is a quick way to get some sexual interaction, a self-esteem boost, or credibility as a person who buys into the social norm that hookup culture sets up. "Being perceived as hooking up can make you look popular and desirable," said one young woman. "I think it's more about the image [than] actually hooking up."

The brevity of a hookup also serves to show how casual a person is about his or her partner. Many students believe they are supposed to regard the hookup as casual—short, and useful, like an afternoon snack for warding off hunger or a workout for staying in shape. Extreme brevity gets sex off one's "To Do" list, and for men, means faster gains in the numbers. Sleepovers and walks of shame are still practiced a fair amount, but the goal remains to avoid any morning interaction. A student leaves before the partner wakes up, ideally, so the social contract of not caring about one's partner can be more easily maintained.

The third, final, and most important criterion that defines a hookup, the presupposition that it will be purely physical and emotionally vacant, is supposed to be sacrosanct. A hookup is a sexual act that thwarts meaning, purpose, and relationship.

Its only function is to provide physical stimulation—maybe to both parties, maybe just one—and in some cases, students will say that it provides pleasure to neither participant. The two partners might not ever know whether the other person enjoyed it, because each person is there, theoretically, only for herself or himself. Worrying about the partner and his or her pleasure will complicate things—so it's better not to ask.

If a person brackets all emotions and feelings of attachment, a hookup becomes an efficient form of sexual interaction. Today's students tend to be overcommitted and extremely busy, and they don't have time (or at least are socialized to believe they don't have time) to get serious about any one person. A hookup is quick, ostensibly meaningless sexual intimacy, so there's no muss and no fuss. Each person enters into the encounter with the expectation that there will be no expectations. Both know why they are there, and it's not for conversation, caring, or hope for a future.

Emotional entanglement is not only not part of the deal, it is verboten, going against the very nature of a hookup. Men and women learn to shut down emotionally in order to "safely" turn on physically. It can take a considerable amount of effort to ward off connection when there is sexual intimacy. Participants train themselves to erase (or at least try to erase) any trace of emotional intimacy, so that they can prevent attachment arising from a sexual encounter. To remain emotionally unscathed, one must develop this skill. The hope is to be able to act like whatever was shared the evening before matters not at all by the morning light. In fact, being "safe" within hookup culture is less about safe sex and more about being able to walk away from sex without any trace of an emotional tug.

This practice creates a drastic divide between physical intimacy and emotional intimacy. If a person goes into a hookup hoping for something more, that's *their* problem, since everybody knows why they are really there. In a way, one can liken a hookup to masturbating with another person present. The problem is, most students fail at this goal, walking away with feelings for their partner.

One young man, a junior from a private-secular university, spoke at length about how people try hard not to care about the people they hook up with. Things still get complicated, he said. One of the partners often develops feelings for the other person. "Most of the time [people] are ambivalent about it—if it was understood by both parties that it's just that [a hookup] and not more," he said. "But I think that's not the case a lot of times, because I think people do get either emotionally invested, or they physically regret it . . . if you're doing that with somebody you don't even know or don't even care about. And as far as emotions go, if one person is more invested in it than the other person, then that's going to cause regret for at least one party."

If a person finds it easy to shut down emotionally while engaging in sexual activity, there is the worry that the other partner may not be equally adept at doing so; if one has trouble turning off one's emotions, the ensuing days will be even more difficult. One young woman who identified as lesbian said, "With a lot of my friends, there's not the pregnancy scare and not the disease scare that there should be," she said. "They're not like 'Oh, no, I had unprotected sex!' It's more like, 'What emotional drama am I going to get into because I had sex with this person? Is she going to call all the time, [or] is she not going to call at all, [or] is this pointless?'" The biggest question of all for this young woman and her friends following a hookup was: "Does she really think she's gay?"

Another important nuance is that even though the hookup is supposed to be about purely physical gratification, that gratification is often in reality a secondary goal—and not only because students hope for something more to come out of the experience. So much of hookup culture is not about what happens in that brief, "emotionless" encounter of sexual intimacy, be it kissing to oral, anal, or vaginal sex. For many, the satisfaction of the hookup is reached only after the physical encounter has ended. The physical piece serves as the experience necessary so students can say to their peers that they had it— so they can feel that, yes, they indeed fit in on campus; that yes, they are a true college student according to today's standards; that yes, they are normal.

"It's something that you know you should do, you should get out there," explained a senior woman from a secular school. "Maybe you'll end up meeting somebody even after you hook up with them. Maybe something more meaningful will evolve out of it. . . . It's just something that I feel like as a college student you're *supposed* to do. It's so ingrained in college life that if you're not doing it, then you're not getting the full college experience." The memory of the hookup, the fact of it, functions as social capital. The significance of bracketing emotional attachment to become sexually active is supposed to serve both partners the following day—it puts them both in a good position to gossip about the experience with their friends, to dissect it with those friends, and perhaps even to exchange vulgarities about their partner as if they don't care about the person even a little.

However, though feelings of emotional investment must be repressed, if not altogether erased, during a hookup, for some students there is an indirect emotional payoff attached to the experience. This comes from the attention they get from the hookup. It positions them with friends and acquaintances in a different way. It can help them climb the social ladder, enable them to make new friends, or allow them to become more popular. The fact of the physical intimacy—that it allows a person to claim it happened—and often the significance of the person with whom it happened, too, can make an enormous difference to a college student's social life.

Not all hookups follow the guidelines set out by the three criteria. Besides the "classic hookup," for example, there is the "serial hookup." Occasionally, a pattern between hookup partners develops—you hook up with the same person over and over again for upward of many months. Serial hookups are kept "random" between two partners—that is, the hookups are never "planned" in the usual sense. The students may start the night out with their respective friends, with everyone getting drunk before the party (pre-gaming), and then get even more trashed at the party, but eventually they run into each other, maybe sometime past midnight, and hook up. This pattern is repeated a week later, or a couple of weeks later, and so on. Sometimes a serial hookup will develop into a relationship down the road. In fact, it is the most common way into a relationship on campus today. A classic hookup will turn into a serial hookup, and six months later the two partners will at last admit that they like each other. The next step is to make a plan to *begin* the night together sober, as opposed to simply running into each other after the party and once they are drunk.

For all intents and purposes, the hookup has replaced the first date on campus. When you encounter college couples today, chances are they got into their committed relationship through a serial hookup. This also means it is likely they had sex before they ever went out on a date or had a serious conversation about their feelings for each other. And it almost certainly means that the couple engaged in many drunken encounters before ever becoming sexually intimate while sober. In this culture, the sex comes first, then openness and communication, but only much, much later.

Chapter Two

The All-Purpose Alcohol Solution

*If you're a girl, you're supposed to get real wasted
and make out with as many people as you want to.*

—FIRST-YEAR WOMAN AT A PUBLIC UNIVERSITY

*The appeal [of parties] is . . . that you lose
self-consciousness. You aren't always regretting
something, you are not always planning for the
future, what am I going to do afterward.
For those moments when you are intoxicated,
you just are not self-conscious.*

—JUNIOR WOMAN AT A
NONRELIGIOUS PRIVATE UNIVERSITY

MOST STUDENTS ARE ABLE TO READILY define how hookups function as social capital on campus—and their definitions are fairly uniform across different institution types. However, many students report what they believe the practice entails *according to everyone else*, as if they did not participate in the practice themselves. When discussing their personal experiences, they often admit they have failed to uphold the social contract of hookup culture, particularly the part about shutting out emotions. Admitting this failure causes them an enormous amount of stress.

For several years, hookup culture is their home. It is everywhere they look and everywhere they go—it *is* their social lives. But eventually, most reject it. It is common for students to have a "wake-up" experience during their sophomore, junior, or senior years, when they realize that they are exhausted, physically and emotionally. They feel emptied out. They become aware that life in hookup culture denies them the experience of meaningful sex and romance. This emotional dissonance is common among both women and men. Students know the deal, they enter into the deal, and then they come away from it, not quite able to uphold the deal. "I thought that [a hookup] was what I wanted the night before," said one young woman. "After a few hookups (and morning-afters), I realized it doesn't feel as good if you don't care about the person and don't think he cares about you. It can be fun, but hooking up is sex without the intimacy, which I think is more important."

Even though students know that emotional intimacy is not supposed to be a part of this deal, many claim they hook up to feel close to another person. They are lonely and want some sort of companionship that seems deeper than casual acquaintance. They realize their behavior is paradoxical, given how they themselves define the hookup. "I don't do well when

I'm single, so I just need to find a guy, which is terrible," said one young woman, a junior at a secular institution. "I would hook up with people just to feel that closeness. I've never regretted anything, and I did like [my partners]—they were nice. But you are never going to find that person you are looking for by hooking up. Maybe it is for some people, but it's not for me."

"It's going to sound depressing, but the motivation for hooking up usually stem[s] from self-esteem problems," said another young woman, also a junior at a secular school. "I feel like a lot of the time . . . people hook up . . . because they want to feel that closeness with someone. And they feel like they don't have it elsewhere. Even if they do, their perception of it is that they don't. They need to have that interaction with someone to make them feel loved. And I think that is the wrong way to go about [things] because when it's done, you just feel the same way again."

Sometimes it sounds as though on the morning after a party the students are all outside sitting on the quad with daisies, plucking petals one at a time, not quite knowing whether they feel like or dislike until that final petal determines the official outcome. This ambivalent, "I liked it, no I didn't, no wait, did I or didn't I?" debate is common, as though students' feelings were not their own to know or decide. One young man reflected this confusion: "A series of thoughts," he wrote. "Sometimes I feel really proud of myself. When I look at my partner, I often think (dependent on partner):

I did *THAT*? [or] Pretty. [or] Eh. [or] This again?" He continued, "Quite often, I just feel a bit empty. This isn't how Disney raised us to believe. As for my actions, they were always clumsy and stupid, but that's part of what makes the humiliating grin fun the day after."

In our idealized Hollywood culture of romance and happy endings, this student noted, the hookup is not what kids are raised to expect of a romantic encounter. The combination of wearing a grin on one's face while feeling empty inside, and describing one's actions as "clumsy and stupid," seems emblematic of the hookup experience. The empty, humiliating grin is part and parcel of what hookup culture is like for students: you must smile in public about it, even if what you did is emptying you out emotionally.

The cost of hooking up is high, and students need something to brick up all of that vacancy inside. Regardless of what students brag about or tell their friends, most are terrible at shutting out the emotional dimensions of sexual intimacy. Yet they feel as if they have to pick themselves up from such dark epiphanies and carry on as though nothing is wrong. Most simply don't have enough self-confidence to find another way of socializing on campus. Since there *appears* to be such widespread support of hookup culture, students are too nervous to openly dissent for fear of being left out. The "lessons" of hookup culture set students back when it comes to pursuing a relationship with someone whom, in another world, they would have liked to ask out on a date. Hookup culture doesn't teach students anything about how to handle the hollow feeling that so many of them wake up to the next morning. In order to keep themselves in the game, students learn to self-medicate.

During the six years that I worked in student affairs—four of them in first-year halls and the remaining two in apartment complexes for sophomores, juniors, and seniors—I had a unique window into college life. During the day, when students were on their way to their classes, I saw them at their best and brightest, freshly showered, and ready to learn. Much of the programming in the residence halls helps to showcase their talents, be they academic, leadership-oriented, or in the performing arts, and the students shine. On weekend nights, they get dressed up and gorgeous before heading out to parties and other social events. Most significant of all: during the day, they are sober.

Then comes the unbelievable amount of drinking that goes on among the students after dark. Many of those same students who shined during the day would return to the residence hall late at night as changed individuals. I would see students coming home so trashed they could barely walk. On Fridays and Saturdays, in the packed elevators among the screaming, drunken masses, there were always a few couples who were sloppy and making out as if they were alone, pressed against each other and too out of it to notice everyone else or to care. By 3 a.m., a parade of students would be doing their best to make it back to one of their rooms without falling down or throwing up before they arrived. Students stumbled into the building in droves, zigzagging along, almost unable to see in front of them or recognize their own friends. Sometimes they were screaming and giggling, but many were belligerent and destructive, tearing through the corridors breaking things, ripping down posters from bulletin boards, and swiping decorations from people's doors only to throw up in front of their own. I've lived in halls where drunken students have set fire to the paper advertisements posted on the walls and thrown large objects, such as televisions, chairs, and mirrors, onto the street or courtyard below, endangering the lives of passersby. Alcohol can transform the politest, nicest students into people who commit shocking, reckless, and dangerous behaviors. It also functions as that X factor of hookup culture, the ingredient that students turn to in order to overcome their hesitation.

There are many studies about alcohol on college campuses. These studies generally look at overall consumption, frequency of consumption, the size of the drinking population at different universities, and the effects of alcohol on student decision-making and sexual activity. In a 2008 study published in the journal *Adolescence*, approximately 25 percent of college students reported that they had recently engaged in binge drinking. Other studies have reported even higher numbers of binge drinkers on campus, with figures of up to 40 percent. According to the *Adolescence* study, about another 30 percent of the students reported frequent social drinking, and 12 percent reported occasional social drinking. The percentages were higher for women than for men in each category. All of this means that more than half of the campus population drinks regularly. These trends were very evident in my study as well. Talk of hookup culture almost inevitably led to talk of alcohol and getting drunk.[1]

During my one-on-one interviews with students, it quickly became clear that there was nothing subtle about the amount of alcohol consumed on campus every weekend. The relationships between drinking and the party scene, and between alcohol and hookup culture, was impossible to miss. There was a pervasive perception among students not only that everyone was drinking, but that everyone was drinking *hard*, that is, drinking in order to get wasted, and that the getting-wasted part had its purpose, too: to ease a person into the mood necessary for a hookup. Perhaps not surprisingly, most of the students with whom I spoke said they did not drink in this manner—much as in the *Adolescence* study. Students would readily admit that they were *around* alcohol regularly, and that they drank some, but they tended to see excessive alcohol consumption as something others did, rather than as something they did themselves—at least not as something they did very often.

Common answers to survey questions about the nature of college social life often cited alcohol. "The number one activity probably on most campuses is drinking," said one first-year man at a Catholic school. A sophomore woman, also on a

Catholic campus, said, "At night . . . a good majority of this campus goes out and drinks." When pressed to say more about why people drank so much, this same young woman attributed it to the challenges of the higher education experience today. "I think part of it is being in college, it's such a stressful time, there's so much going on, there's so many expectations required," she explained. "And, [drinking is] a chance to relax from all that and hang out with friends and to be able to let loose. I think for some people it's an escape—to get away from things that are really bothering them. But I think a lot of it is just that people are really stressed."

One young man, also a first-year student at a Catholic college, had only one word for me when I asked what people usually did on the weekends at his school: "Drink." Yet he went on to say that, although he did participate a little, he felt that he was different in his drinking habits from everybody else on campus. "I do [drink] sometimes, but I am very moderate with it. Where[as] a lot of people came here and as soon as they had that freedom, they ran with it." When asked why alcohol was so appealing to people on his campus, he, too, distanced himself from the sort of drinking he believed everyone else was doing. "Alcohol can be a catalyst for conversation," he said. "Like something mind-altering can spark some kind of imagination. But some people abuse it completely, and feel compelled to do it every night of the week. I don't really admire that in anyone. It's upsetting to see a lot of kids falling into it."

This student's comment about alcohol as a "catalyst for conversation" was really a veiled statement about how students hook up. Most of the students I interviewed stated this more plainly, such as a sophomore woman from a Catholic college, who said, "I think that alcohol is the catalyst of finally making [something into] an intimate relationship. [Alcohol] just makes it easier. You would never walk up to someone and just start making out with them if you weren't intoxicated. It makes your inhibitions go." A male student who was a junior at a secular university cited alcohol as *the* determining factor in hookup culture. Without alcohol, he said, hookup culture wouldn't even exist.

This student also said that first-year students, in particular, were fixated on expectations to hook up and used alcohol to get themselves into the right mindset. "Alcohol flows much easier here than it did at home in high school," he explained. "So when people are drunk their inhibitions are let go—that's just common knowledge—and people feel freer to use alcohol as an excuse or as the real reason why they're feeling less inhibited to be promiscuous." These types of comments seem to be corroborated by the evidence. According to a 2007 study published in the journal *Addictive Behaviors*, 32 percent of students reported having unprotected sex after drinking. Overall, the study showed that a whopping 55 percent of the sexual encounters on campus with someone who was not a steady partner involved alcohol.[2]

Alcohol is key to the perpetuation of hookup culture on campus. It plays a huge part in the poor decisions students often make—and later regret. At evangelical colleges, which are dry, and where only a tiny sliver of the population breaks the rules by drinking and partying, hookup culture—at least as students at Catholic, private-secular, and public institutions know it—simply does not exist.[3] Although it would be difficult to establish a definitive causal relationship between drinking culture and hookup culture, the correlation, at least, seems fairly obvious.

But is *everyone* on campus really getting wasted and hooking up? In my interviews and online survey, the "me vs. everyone else" motif was quite prominent. Students talked about alcohol as if it were an all-powerful, extremely pervasive factor on campus affecting everyone's behavior—everyone *else's* behavior, at least. They did not often believe it was an important factor in their own behavior.

One of the online survey questions asked how often it had been the case that when a student had engaged in sexual activity, he or she had also been drinking alcohol or using a drug (see Table 2.1). Nearly a quarter of the students answering this question responded that they had "never" drunk alcohol or used drugs during sexual activity. Also, more than a quarter answered they had "rarely" drunk or used drugs during sexual activity. Together these respondents represented more than 50 percent of the students who took the online survey. This still left approximately 48 percent of the students.

TABLE 2.1: Survey Data
Sexual Activity and Use of Alcohol or Drugs

How often is it the case when you have engaged in sexual activity that you have also been drinking alcohol or using a drug?	Response Percent	Response Count (776 students)
Never	24.5%	190
Rarely	27.3%	212
More often had not been drinking or using a drug	20.6%	160
Equal times had been drinking or using a drug as not	11.9%	92
More often had been drinking or using a drug than not	9.4%	73
Frequently	4.8%	37
All the time	1.5%	12

These students admitted in the survey that they had been drinking or using a drug at least some of the time when they had been engaging in sexual activity. Forty-eight percent is a significant number, certainly, but it is a far cry from "everybody." Thus, if we assume that the students who took the survey were accurately reporting their own use of alcohol and drugs during sexual activity, we can see that there is a fairly significant discrepancy between perceptions of the correlation between alcohol use and sexual activity and the reality.

One likely interpretation of these results is that students simply lie to their peers about all sorts of things—whether they are still a virgin, how many times they've hooked up (men up their numbers, women do the opposite), and exactly how drunk they were the night before when they engaged in x, y, and z. Alcohol has always been the great excuse for all sorts of behavior, but never before have students been so dependent on it to explain away their sexual encounters, both to others and to themselves. The incentive to either be, or at least appear to be, drunk on Thursday, Friday, and Saturday nights is high. Saying that you were drunk when you did something—even if you were not—will often get you a pass from peers. The shock of what someone did the night before—how far they went, who they were with, where they did whatever it was they did—can be lessened or even waved away if a person can say they were trashed at the time. Admitting to sobriety makes a person more fully responsible for his or her behavior.[4]

The student I interviewed who cited alcohol as the determining factor in hookup culture, like many other students, felt that alcohol was a key ingredient of the hookup because it allowed people to excuse themselves from responsibility for whatever sexual intimacy occurred. The first time this young man had had sex was during a hookup. "Alcohol went into the decision," he said about this experience. "I guess [my partner and I] just started hooking up and started having unprotected sex and then I just stopped and said [to myself], 'Wait, what am I doing? This is stupid!' But then I kind of blocked it out of my memory for a while."

I heard many similar stories. It's disconcerting to listen to so many students talk about how they relinquished their agency for sexual decision-making because of alcohol. This young man's stammering phrases of "I guess" and "I just," and the way he reported blocking out what had happened—his claim to confusion, in other words—were revealing. They showed that he was trying to justify his behavior and absolve himself of responsibility because he was drunk. The way he described this sexual encounter made it sound as if he had suddenly woken up and was surprised to find himself in bed with a woman, as if the alcohol had acted of its own accord and without his consent. This kind of talk begs consideration of the nature of sexual consent itself within hookup culture. Is there indeed a relationship between drinking and the hookup that diminishes a person's sexual agency? And, if so, what does "consent" mean here? How does one give consent to have sex if so many people use alcohol to relinquish responsibility for whatever "happens"?

In general, my survey data and the narratives of the students show that although students appear to revel in hookup culture when in public, in private they admit that much of the sexual activity in hookups is unwanted, at worst, and ambivalent, at best.

When alcohol is the self-medicating medium of choice, the conversation about sexual assault becomes very complicated. The 41 percent of students in my survey who reported being profoundly upset about hooking up said the encounters made them feel, among other things, used, miserable, disgusted, and duped. Most disturbing of all were those who likened their hookups to "abuse." Within hookup culture, it is too simplistic to have conversations about date rape and "no means no," since this culture is one that by definition *excludes dating*, almost prohibiting it, while promoting using copious amounts of alcohol. Taken together, it has students not only *not* saying no, but barely saying anything at all, including yes.

Researchers have begun to investigate the relationship between alcohol consumption, sexual assault, and hookup culture on campus. An article in the *Journal of Interpersonal Violence* found that, with respect to alcohol consumption generally, 41 percent of student participants drank one to two times per week, and 28 percent drank more than twice per week. Fifty-six percent of these students said that when they drank, their intention was to get drunk. These statistics are perhaps not surprising, given the way American culture glorifies drinking on college campuses. Yet, according to these researchers, the prevalence of hooking up drastically increased when alcohol was involved, as did the prevalence of unsafe sex and sexual assault. The study showed that 62 percent of unwanted sex occurred because the student's "judgment was impaired due to drugs and alcohol."[5]

In a follow-up study in the same journal, researchers claimed that approximately 26 percent of college students in their first and second years of college had had sex with someone they had just met when they were under the influence of alcohol; 40.4 percent had had sex with someone they knew, but with whom they were not in a relationship, while under the influence of alcohol. The accompanying statistics on sexual assault on campus in this study were startling. Approximately 44 percent of the women participating in the study reported at least one unwanted sexual encounter while in college, and 90 percent of this unwanted sex took place during a hookup. Of all the reported incidents of unwanted sex, 76.2 percent involved alcohol, which played a significant role in blurring the lines of consent. The researchers found that often, the victim was too drunk to properly give consent. Often, the victim did not really remember what had happened after waking up the next day.[6]

Several of the young women I interviewed discussed how, during a hookup, it did not occur to their partners to ask for— or even wait for—consent. Talking is not what the hookup is about—getting it done is. Though these women knew (more or less) that they had not said yes to sexual intimacy, they were also unwilling to call it sexual assault. Instead, they called on ambiguous language to avoid the claim. "I didn't actually say no in the situation, it just kind of happened," said one young woman. "I didn't want to do it," she went on, but then later added, "I don't feel like he raped me, but it *was* against my will the first time." Another woman described having first-time sex during high school with someone who was "just a normal guy," yet who forced her to have sex because it was "what he thought [she] wanted." He didn't actually ask her what she wanted, let alone wait for an answer. "Sometimes I wonder if it was rape or if I really wanted it and wanted acceptance," she said, looking back on the event. "I'd be lying if I said I wasn't struggling with it, but I feel a lot of it is [my] intent." By intent, this young woman meant, "her fault" for allowing it to "just happen."[7]

When alcohol explicitly entered into the situation, claiming an encounter as sexual assault didn't seem to even occur to anyone as a possibility. One young woman wrote in her journal about a disturbing experience she'd had. She regretted the experience, but she did not name it for what it was, going so far as to blame herself for what happened because she'd been so drunk at the time. "When we went to bed, we began to hook up, and I was obviously not in the state to be doing so," she began. "The next thing I know I was giving him oral sex. He was basically masturbating into my mouth because I was too drunk to do anything more than hold my mouth there." This young woman was so out of it that not only was she unable to consent, she was too drunk to move away when someone was "masturbating into her mouth." That this sexual assault went unreported by her is a given—a big part of what hookup culture teaches both women and men on campus is that "sex just happens," especially when you're drunk. The goal is to avoid crying about it the next day, since that creates drama and therefore defeats the purpose of the hookup.

In April 2011, the Obama administration issued a letter out of the US Department of Education's Office of Civil Rights to all university and college administrators requiring them to better uphold the existing policies regarding sexual assault on campus under Title IX. The colleges were told to expand their prevention efforts and improve sexual-assault investigations.[8] The letter, issued in response to the alarming statistics of sexual assault among college women, was hard-hitting and extensive in its outline and interpretation of Title IX policy. Clearly, the Obama administration views sexual assault as a problem that is growing worse on American campuses. The letter concluded by proposing possible solutions and emphasized victim's rights and protection. Though the letter stopped short of requiring specific programming, it strongly recommended that colleges develop their own unique response to its call, with campus-wide educational programs to include faculty, staff, administrators, and coaches. The letter included recommendations for defining sexual harassment and sexual assault and distributing this information widely on campus, as well as the need for counseling victims and anyone emotionally affected by any campus incidents.

This is the first time that all colleges and universities in the United States have publicly been taken to task on the issue of sexual assault on campus at such a high level and in such a comprehensive way. This letter said there is no longer any getting out of addressing sexual assault on campus—a grand victory for all students and those who care about their well-being. Since the letter first appeared, as I've traveled the country on the lecture circuit, I've encountered administrators and faculty preparing to meet Obama's call with admirable zeal. Most of them feel empowered by the mandate, having already spent many years seeking permission to address this issue but being held back by nervous superiors and board members worried about scandal or simply waving off assault as a non-problem.

I am encouraged by the hard line taken by the Obama administration with colleges on this issue. My cheer is tempered, however, by my worry that the vast majority of campuses will fail to address hookup culture's very intimate relationship to the topic—a failure that could wipe out so much of the good that could (and should) result from this call to deal with sexual assault. Most college campuses have either barely contended with hookup culture, or, as with sexual assault in the past, have altogether waved off the conversation, either because of potential scandal, because it's surely not a problem on *their* campus, or because they don't regard it as a problem, period. Most sexual-assault programming I've encountered during campus visits still centers on language—*no means no* and *yes means yes*—and the importance of gaining consent. This type of education is absolutely imperative and significant to the conversation, yet in so many ways it has also become useless in light of hookup culture.

Hooking up is a practice where communication itself is eschewed as destructive to the success of the activity. When such a practice exists, then attacking a related problem—sexual assault, in this case—with education that depends on a student's ability and willingness to communicate is perhaps not the best tactic. This, of course, does not mean this type of education should be dropped. But I worry that in our national discussion of hookup culture on campus, the two issues—the hookup and the sexual assault—might not be addressed together. And they must be addressed together if we are to put a stop to sexual assault. One of the most productive conversations we could have is the conversation about how we can educate people about sexual assault on campus and address this issue in light of a widespread culture that teaches students that yes and no are irrelevant, that they should be apathetic about sexual intimacy, and that whatever happens under the influence of alcohol is unavoidable and justified.

Chapter Three

Opting In to a Culture of Casual Sex

I think [oral sex] is very casual . . .
a step beyond making out. It's nothing too big.
—FIRST-YEAR STUDENT AT A CATHOLIC COLLEGE

Being a virgin is a negative thing—it's like,
something to be corrected.
—SOPHOMORE MAN AT A PRIVATE-SECULAR UNIVERSITY

"ORAL SEX IS LIKE, THE ULTIMATE whatever," said a young woman named Maggie during a one-on-one interview. A senior attending a secular university, she displayed a carefully crafted, laid-back, almost ambivalent attitude about all things related to sex. "I think it would make just as little difference if someone heard in gossip that someone made out with someone or that they had oral sex. It's almost the exact same thing."

Maggie was one of many students who spoke of how common oral sex had become among college students, and sometimes high-school students, too. Oral sex, one young man from a private-secular university told me, was a pretty common occurrence during a hookup—a girl giving and a guy receiving, that is. He wondered why there was a gender imbalance here. "A lot of [oral sex is] a social thing or almost a social expectation, which is terrible. I don't know where it started or where it comes from, maybe just from if girls feel more insecure or if they feel like they have to do it to make a guy happy. But I think that's definitely the trend."

William, another young man from a private-secular university, talked at length about the blasé attitudes of his peers about oral sex. People acted like it was not a big deal—not in comparison to *sexual*-sex, as he put it. "While hooking up, to have oral sex, it's almost expected. It doesn't have the emotional undertones of sex. For a lot of people, it's almost a cop-out. People have these urges and they are trying to satisfy them, and they don't want to commit to having sexual-sex, or a relationship where you are having sex with someone, so they do the next best thing." Girls, he said, were not normally on the pleasurable end of oral sex. "I think it's socially more acceptable for men to receive . . . and I know a lot of my guy friends are doing a lot more receiving than giving."

Susan, a soft-spoken senior from a secular university, said oral sex was exceedingly popular on campus, precisely because "people think about it as being not real sex." She was quick to comment about how this perspective was dangerous because having oral sex was just as risky as any other kind of genital contact in terms of STIs (a topic that both Maggie and William eventually brought up as well). Susan worried that many people at her college believed that oral sex was less dangerous than intercourse, but that this attitude made oral sex even more dangerous than other types of sex because it promoted reckless behavior. Like William and others, Susan said that girls were most at risk for STIs because they were the most likely to be the "givers."

Susan thought that girls were more desperate to please men than men were to please women, more desperate for a relationship than men were, and more likely than men to hope that a hookup might turn into something long term, even though this expectation went against the social contract of the hookup. This "desperation" both worried and saddened her. She felt that girls were willing to perform an act that gave them little reward or pleasure because they tended to see the possibility of a relationship resulting from the hookup. Or, "maybe [it was] just because *guys* are unwilling" to become the givers that girls were stuck with this task.

If oral sex was no big deal, then was "sexual-sex" a big deal? For so many of the students with whom I spoke, the answer was no. Most of them could still be surprised by a person's virginity—even stunned—and more so if that person was also gay or lesbian. "I don't think people think there are virgins anymore," said Jenna, a senior at a secular university who identified as lesbian and considered herself a virgin. "Especially in the LGBT community, I have two friends who are virgins also and we call ourselves the three V's. It's because people believe if you have another sexual orientation, it's because you've had other sexual experiences. I don't think people realize people are still virgins." According to Jenna, gay guys experience even more pressure on this front. "We somehow expect guys to get all this game when they're out," she said. "In the LGBT community, you always hear about the token gay guy and people asking him, 'How many guys did you get last night?' People expect them to be with so many guys."

For some students, learning that a peer was still a virgin was a much bigger deal than hearing that people had oral sex. "I think it's always shocking to find out that someone's a virgin," said Maggie. "You're like, 'Really?!'" By the time a person gets to college today, it's expected that they've had sex. It's considered odd if someone hasn't, and possibly a problem—a big one. "I think it's bad to find out that someone you're interested in or involved with is a virgin, because [you think], 'Oh my god, I know that this is going to mean more to you than it is to me.' My first boyfriend when I got to college—I was seventeen and he was twenty-one, and he was a virgin and I wasn't—that freaked me out a lot. My friends and I don't *really* care. It's just that initial moment, when you find out, is shocking."

The first time Maggie had sex, she was in high school, and she took the experience and its aftermath very seriously, at least until she got to college. At the time, she was in a long-term relationship with someone about whom she cared deeply. "It was a really big decision," she explained. "It was my senior year in high school and I had just turned seventeen. I made the decision in October that I was ready for it, and it didn't take place until after Christmas. It was a really, *really* big deal for me."

Even though Maggie put so much thought into having sex that first time, she was still nervous about STIs and had a guilty Catholic conscious. "It was coming up on six months that [my boyfriend and I] had been together, and I was finally like, 'Okay, this is what I want to do.' It was at that point [that] the religious factors were a big deal, and also, I was *terrified* of getting pregnant. So I had to sneak into the Planned Parenthood behind my parents' back and get birth control, take every possible precaution. I was really, really scared of (a) people finding out, and (b) getting pregnant. Once it was sure that neither of those two things were going to happen, then I was ready to do it."

In retrospect, Maggie thought she made a bigger deal about it than she should have. "I think it is hard to wait, but more than that, I think it's unnecessary to wait," she said. "I don't know about most people my age, but I don't plan to get married until I'm at least late twenties, early thirties, so to me [waiting] doesn't make any sense, because when people were saying, 'Save yourself for marriage,' they were getting married straight out of high school or straight out of college. That's not how it is anymore."

Maggie's high-school friends knew about the night she lost her virginity and all the thinking that had gone into the decision. But even years later, Maggie's parents still had no idea, and she had no plans to tell them. When it came to getting advice about sex, Maggie went to two different sets of friends for counsel, her high-school friends and her college friends. "I get all my relationship advice from one group of friends and all my sex advice from another group of friends," Maggie wrote in her journal, clarifying that all of these friends were girls. She wrote:

> Each group has a different set of values that serves each topic better. My high-school friends are the relationship people— they want to know who I'm dating and how it's going. They ask questions that are more long-term oriented and advise me to seek out meaningful relationships rather than date around. My college friends are the ones I talk to about sex. I don't have to apologize to them for drunken hookups and sexual misadventures. They are constantly warning me about guys getting too attached, or keeping myself at a distance. They advise me to hold my cards close and play them strategically to get what I want. I need both of these groups to balance each other in my life.

Maggie's observations about her friends reflect a larger issue common among students at the university level—there are hookups in high school, sure, but relationships are common in high school, too. The kind of support Maggie associated with her college friends was about freedom from judgment about drunken sexual encounters that ruled out relationship. "Misadventures" seemed to be Maggie's term for her hookups, for sexual encounters she felt insecure about, and even for encounters she felt ashamed about. Her college friends shored up the notion that "hookups are totally okay" even if you don't like them, if you feel bad about them, and if you wish you hadn't engaged in them after the fact. It is friends like these that help perpetuate hookup culture on campus. These friends probably also feel ambivalent and uncomfortable about hookups, yet they learn to put on a good game face for their friends and peers.

The fact that Maggie went to her high-school friends to talk about dating and anything "long-term oriented" or potentially "meaningful" reveals an important difference between high school and college when it comes to the culture of sex. Many students say that finding a relationship during college is nearly impossible because it's all hookups all the time. They frequently say, "Nobody ever dates at my college." The message college students get is that once you start your freshman year, if you're not casual about sex, then you risk sticking out among your peers—and not in a good way. Others see you as immature, uptight, unattractive, and laughably inexperienced.[1] For many students, the kind of shock Maggie expressed that anyone could still be a virgin is exactly what they want to avoid when it comes to what their peers think of them—it's the reason they feel they need to hide the truth about their sexual past, and it can push them into a first-time sexual encounter that they later regret, sometimes for years.

Not all college students, but a large subset of them, were like Maggie in that they believed they were supposed to be hooking up in college, even if they had felt very differently about the role of sexual activity in their lives during high school. For Maggie, the passage from virginity into postvirginity meant losing all the romanticism she had once had about love, commitment, meaning, emotional intimacy, and communication. Hookup culture requires that students become hardened about sex, dropping all those needs and hopes they may have had about its potential romantic dimensions. And once students are no longer a virgins, according to this view, they are "free" to forget about love, meaning, and commitment, "liberated" to have sex with whomever comes along without any strings, "keeping oneself at a distance" from partners and turning to friends for a reality check if they think they might be "getting too attached."

When Maggie moved from "care-full sex" the first time she had it into the "care-free sex" of hookup culture, the lesson she learned was that "misadventures" are par for the course. She didn't get pregnant or contract an STI that first time, so this proved to her that it was fine to let go of her worries and get past all that emotional stuff the next time, and the time after that. Not being a virgin by the time a person is a senior in college is a relief, because virginity is considered off-putting—it implies that someone cares far more about sex than hookup culture dictates they should. And once someone has moved beyond first-time sex, they are supposed to become ambivalent about sex on every level.

It is notable that student perceptions of their peers' attitudes about sex—that "everyone" is casual about it during college—

are off-base. Of the 1,230 students who answered an optional question for the online survey about what they thought *their peers* thought about sex on campus, 45 percent of students at Catholic schools and 36 percent at nonreligious private and public schools said their peers were *too* casual about sex. These students gave answers that distanced themselves from the hookup ethic, claiming that, though their peers did not take sex seriously or were casual about sex, they themselves took sex seriously in a way that distinguished them from everyone else.[2] Said one young man about his peers, "I think that people are *very* in favor of people having sex."

One young woman at a Catholic college spoke at length about her own friends' opinions. She thought that they openly departed from the norm in their attitudes about casual sex on her campus. "They're opposed to the whole casual sex idea, but I think as a whole the campus is open to the idea of casual sex," she said. Plus, she explained, a lot of her friends were still virgins and admitted this, at least to each other. "I don't think there's necessarily pressure to *not* be a virgin," she went on. "But then, there are always going to be guys who are jerks and ridicule you a little bit." This young woman felt that it was pretty unusual to encounter a group of virgin girls like her and her friends, especially when they were seniors, as they were. But the data from the online survey show that virgins are more common than most people think. Thirty-one percent of the girls answering the survey at Catholic and secular universities identified as virgins, as did

33.8 percent of the men, and 21 percent of the seniors answering the survey (men and women) reported they were still virgins.

A similar discrepancy showed up when students were given the opportunity to speak about the meaning of sex for them on a personal level. Even though students were very aware that the social contract for a hookup required them to check their emotions at the door, a large percentage said sexual intimacy was nevertheless a primary vehicle for the very thing hookup culture says sex must be liberated from—attachment. Out of 1,010 students at Catholic and secular institutions who answered a series of questions designed to get at their personal attitudes about sex, 30 percent strongly disagreed that casual sex was acceptable. An additional 20 percent somewhat disagreed that casual sex was acceptable. Together, those students constituted about half the student population answering the question. A whopping 41 percent said they felt strongly that to engage in sex they needed to be in a committed relationship, and another 18 percent simply agreed, for a total of 59 percent of respondents. To the statement, "Sex is primarily the taking of pleasure from another person," 43 percent strongly disagreed and another 32 percent somewhat disagreed—which adds up to about 75 percent of respondents. Thus, three-quarters of the respondents at least appeared to disagree with the notion of hookup sex defined as a purely physical experience. Perhaps the most dissonant response from students showed up in opinions about this statement: "The best sex is with no strings attached." Here, 58 percent of participants strongly disagreed, another 26 percent somewhat disagreed, and only 4 percent either somewhat or strongly agreed.

By the time you are "eighteen, nineteen, twenty," William said, people begin to believe you can engage in meaningful relationships and that you are emotionally mature enough to handle having sex. The perception is that "everyone is ready" at this age, that "everyone [at college] is mature enough" to have sex. But this perception, he said, doesn't measure up to the reality of what people actually experience when they have sex during college. According to William, the peer expectation that everyone is ready for sex, and therefore should be having sex, amounts to a lot of "meaningless sex" and an accompanying lack of meaningful relationships. The perception that people know what they are doing and know how to get into meaningful relationships is a false perception, and one that, at least in William's opinion, leads to a lot of random sexual encounters that don't go anywhere, at least not anywhere very positive. Regardless of whether or not the sex was good, he said, plenty of people would still "shout it from rooftops" that they had hooked up.

In reflecting back on his own hookup experiences at college, William felt a tremendous amount of unease. "At the time when I was hooking up, I did regret it—I had plenty of regret then and I have even more regret now," he said. William's hookups gave him a feeling of missed opportunities, of relationships that could have been but weren't, because a hookup was about *not* talking afterward. "Most of the morning-after experience isn't shared at all between the two parties—it's mostly shared between the person and their friends," he explained about the important role of gossip post-hookup. "Most hookups don't develop into anything, and most of the time it's almost as if the two parties are *expected* to grow apart from each other and [to] no longer come in contact. It's strange that two people could be feeling the same thing and wouldn't necessarily talk about it because it's almost taboo to talk about it, because it *could* mean one thing for one party and be completely different for the other person."

Like William, many students said they went into hookups with the intention of engaging in sexual intimacy without anything further. It wasn't supposed to lead anywhere. Yet, once on the other side of the experience, they felt remorse, and sometimes they felt foolish, as though they had been duped into believing that they could do this, and then found that they could not.

SUSAN, THE STUDENT WHO WORRIED that girls had a "desperation" for relationships that led them to regularly perform oral sex, fluctuated between being happy about having "finally" lost her virginity during a hookup and feeling rather ambivalent about the experience.

"I put a lot of pressure on myself to hurry up and get rid of my virginity," she said. "I felt like it was this big thing that was keeping me from experiencing life, in a weird way. I was getting antsy with doing the whole make-out thing with guys, and I knew people who had had sex and they talked about how great it was. It's a rite of passage and I wanted to hurry up and get there, so I ended up sleeping with somebody that I had had a crush on for a long time, but it didn't turn into a relationship or anything." When I asked Susan whether or not this bothered her, she was up and down about it. "I probably could have made a better choice because he's not the best person. I enjoyed it, I was glad that it happened, and I think that I was mostly glad that this rite of passage had taken place and I was finally into that other world—I didn't really regret that part."

Being "into that other world" for Susan meant she had joined her peers on campus who were sexually active, and she didn't waste time before trying on her new, sexually active self again that next semester. "I started meeting guys and, I'm ashamed of this, but I had a spurt of sleeping with a few different guys," she explained. "I think it was just because I was so happy to be in that place where I could finally do this, because I didn't want the first person I slept with to be somebody random, so I did *that*."

Typically, once students no longer consider themselves virgins, the sex they then have is regarded as lesser—in importance, in meaning, and in the standards they might hold themselves to for choosing partners—than the sex they had that first time. This "once it's gone, it's gone," mentality about virginity often led Susan to think that the sex she had later on didn't matter much, and her comments reflected this. For obvious reasons, this mentality lends itself well to hookup culture. Hookup culture would not exist without it, and it is perpetuated by it. If the only type of sex that is supposed to matter is first-time sex, then all subsequent sex is categorically less significant, just like hookup sex.

Eventually, Susan "slowed down a little bit." She tried to be more relaxed about her sexual encounters and "not as intense" about how she felt about them emotionally—or about the fact that she *did* care emotionally. She went back and forth about how much she told her friends about who she had slept with and how many partners she'd had, just as she went back and forth about how she felt about her actions. "I definitely had spurts where I would regret it, and then I would be like, fine, I don't regret it. . . . I'm glad that I'm not in that place anymore, and part of me regrets it a little bit, but I accept it as it happened, and I'm hoping that I've gotten past that level of immaturity where I would feel the need to do that [sleep with different guys]."

Susan's ambivalence about her sexual experiences in the context of hookup culture was plain. In one moment she decided that she was "fine" about everything she'd done, and in another she spoke of trying to simply "accept it as it happened" even though she felt unease. In this regard she was similar to many other students. Using such language seemed to help many students believe that they were not really agents in their own actions, as if the things they had done were not so much personal choices but experiences that washed over them as they got pulled into the tide of the culture, like so many of their peers.

All the "thats" and the "its" in Susan's statements were interesting, too, as was her reference to "that place" she was no longer in anymore, or "that stage" she believed she had moved beyond. Many women and men at college are eager to enter "that other world" where they are no longer considered virgins. They believe their virginity keeps them from a mysterious, exciting way of being that many of their peers already know. They don't want to be left out. Being a virgin in in the midst of hookup culture makes them feel humiliated, alone, and unwanted. They also tend to describe this culture as an environment where sex "happens" more than it is chosen. But then, for students like Susan, once they finally get to "that other world," where they are "free" to be sexually active people, they do not necessary like "that place" as much as they thought they would. Susan's constant use of "that" was a means of distancing herself from hookup culture, and from her participation in it, since after living there for a few months, she felt tremendously ashamed of her behavior. She concluded our interview with comments that echoed William's, explaining that she hoped she was "past that level of immaturity where [she] would feel the need to do that."

ANOTHER YOUNG WOMAN, Allison, who was a first-year student at a Catholic college, flip-flopped about whether her first sexual experience was a hookup or a more meaningful, planned experience. At the time of our interview, she was still friends with the guy it happened with. "It almost *seems* random," she said, "but it wasn't, because we were with each other and I was in his room, and it just got heated and that's what ended up happening because the relationship was at that point, that's all." Then Allison told me a second time that the sex wasn't planned, that it "just happened," but that this was okay with her because, again, they were still friends.

According to Allison, if having sex was "appropriate," then you didn't have to feel bad or guilty or ashamed about it after the fact, and sex was appropriate when there was "an equal exchange of emotion." When there wasn't an equal exchange, sex became "inappropriate" and she felt regret about it. "I did have a couple of random hookups on two separate occasions and I'm not happy about them," Allison said. "But overall I don't regret my sexual experience when it was appropriate."

Allison spoke of a pervasive attitude at her Catholic college that sex should be casual. "This is going to sound awful, but [sex] is almost a goal," she said. "The general notion on campus is [that] if you're with somebody, or if you're going to a party, the goal for the night is to have that hookup." Allison explained that it felt as though sex "can happen any time," because "it doesn't matter anymore, in this day and age, in what context you have sex, because people are going to do it no matter what—so it will happen with random hookups." Allison kept coming back to this notion that sex was everywhere she turned at her college, which also accounted for why she felt like being a virgin could be a big problem socially.

"Me and my friends were up in the dorm talking about stuff we did in the past—our sexual past," Allison said. "One of the girls in the dorm is a virgin, and she got red in the face because she felt like she couldn't add to the conversation." She explained: "She actually said that—'I can't add to the conversation because I haven't experienced that.' We've partied with her before and we look at her as having a *lack* of experience, as being so innocent. This sounds so much like high school, but if you haven't had sex, you're not cool. There is a stigma against people like that." For Allison, being a virgin could not only make you feel left out, but it really did leave you out, whereas talking about sex, how you wanted to have sex, how you wanted to hook up that night, how your hookup went after the fact, allowed you to claim an acceptable social life on campus. Allison felt that it was crucial to be able to at least "allude to promiscuity," as she put it. Being able to speak to sexual experiences helped put you in the middle of conversations with peers, allowed you to be accepted at parties, and assured you acceptance in general. Without sex, a person would be rather lost socially.

By understanding that having sex is "just what college students do," Allison was able to feel less actively responsible for her own decisions around sex and to convince herself that she was only going with the flow. Like Susan—the young woman who had used the word "that" again and again—Allison used language to distance herself from sexual encounters she wanted to forget. By saying that sex "just happened," or describing how she sort of "got into a situation" where sex seemed like "the right thing to do," Allison was attempting to excuse herself by implying that she did not have full agency over her sexual experiences and decision making.

A common theme throughout my interviews was how, if a person was not sexually active, it could become difficult for them to establish themselves socially on campus, especially if that person was male. Not all students felt this way, but a lot of them, both women and men, complained that being a virgin could make people social outcasts on campus or make them seem old-fashioned or even prudish. Virginity marks the virgin socially, because it limits what that individual is able to do in the context of hookup culture. A virgin's lack of sexual experience can make him or her a taboo hookup partner. The assumption is that any sexual encounter with a virgin is more complicated than an encounter with a non-virgin, especially if the hookup is between a virgin and a non-virgin (rather than two non-virgins). The virgin, it is presumed, will always want something to come of the experience, and the non-virgin, it is presumed, is "past all that stuff." Virgins come with strings, in other words, which goes against the definition of a hookup.

Therefore, many students become sexually active because they think it is socially unacceptable to care about sex—a student's job is to learn to be casual about it and to work on adopting this attitude. The idea that sex is so common during college that it "can happen anytime," as Allison put it, requires a person to stop acting like it's a big deal. With this attitude so prominent among large swaths of the college population, it should come as no surprise that a similarly large population of students feel ambivalent about the sex they've had. They have very strong feelings about the social status of sex on campus, but they are rarely interested in discussing their personal sexual encounters. So, although many students talked at length about having had sex, few mentioned whether or not they had enjoyed any of it. The act becomes largely irrelevant—it is the fact that they can claim the act that matters most.

Hookup culture teaches college students to simply not care about sex at all. But this may be just the opening needed to initiate positive conversations about sex. What might "good sex" look like? And is "good sex" possible in the context of hookup culture? Discussions around these topics might begin to shift student attitudes, guiding them toward better decision-making about the sex they are having and empowering them to opt in, instead, to a sexually active culture where meaningful, pleasurable sex is not merely a possibility far off on the horizon, after a serial hookup is established, but something much closer, a goal they can identify from the very beginning and with a partner who desires the same.

Chapter Four

Learning to Play the Part
(of Porn Star):
The Sexualization of College Girls

Most theme parties are an excuse
for girls to dress really trashy.

—SOPHOMORE WOMAN AT A CATHOLIC COLLEGE

AMERICAN HIGH-SCHOOL CULTURE has always loved to categorize girls according to presumed sexual histories and reputations. There are the Good Girls, who are appropriately, sexually restrained with boys, who only go out with "nice boys," and who stay away from the "players" who might tarnish their reputations. There are the "holier than thou" girls, the Prudes, who stay away from boys to protect themselves from being sullied by them, and who seem sexually repressed. Then there are the Sluts, the girls who "give themselves away" all the time, offering sex for "free" because they expect nothing from their partners other than a night of sex. The Good Girl is both envied and hated for being so perfect. Everyone waits for the Prude to fall because they know she'll fall hard. The Slut is scorned and treated like trash.

No one wins with such categories. The Good Girl is happy about her status, yet she is stuck in it, too. She never gets to play the part of the Slut, even if she envies the Slut's seeming freedom to do what she wants, because if the Good Girl slips up even one night, her reputation is tarnished. The Slut can do whatever she wants, with whomever she wants, but really, what does this freedom get her, and how did she get there in the first place? The Slut was likely one of the Good Girls who "slipped up" one night and hooked up with a boy who boasted, and suddenly her careful reputation was ruined forever. She is stuck, too. Now she goes along with the part everyone's cast her in. She becomes the Slut for real, because what other choice does she have? And the Prude, well, she may be pure, but no one thinks she has any fun, or *is* any fun, for that matter. The Prude is stuck sitting up in her tower room where no one can reach her, and no one bothers to try. But there she remains, waiting for Prince Charming to scale those walls and rescue her.

Then there is that unforgiving, age-old system that perpetuates these roles and their corresponding narratives. The girls (mostly) who gossip about everybody and make those labels stick. The avenues for spreading gossip, which are ever more expansive and unforgiving because of technology, with Facebook, Twitter, and other social media working to both create and ruin everyone's reputations, but especially those of young women. Today, a girl can go from Prude to Slut at lightning speed. Being in the wrong place at the wrong time and getting caught in a compromising situation can cost a girl a lot more today than it would have in the past, because someone may well snap a photo and publicize it for all the world to see. High school no longer knows any boundaries; photos, videos, and comments go viral far beyond the students at one school. Old-style gossip limited to the people in one's town or immediate peer group seems quaint in comparison. When these girls go to college, their reputations are reset, as long as they've escaped the tyranny of the technological tarnish.

But it is at this point that today's college culture throws them a new archetype, one that takes a nod from these three popular stereotypes, mashing them together, and adds the heavy influence of pornography.

In the pornography industry, the male sexual fantasy is typically performed with the man always in the position of power and authority. He has all the control, which is represented by his position and attire—he wears a jacket and tie as the respectful, successful executive, or he is in football gear, making him literally larger than life. At the very least, a man is typically fully clothed in an outfit that would be acceptable at work or in public. The woman's role is the exact opposite—she's powerless, submissive, and, most of all, dependent on him for something, whether it's her job (she's his secretary), her grade (his student), or his knowledge so she can do her job (she's the nurse, not the doctor), and so on. The woman (or the girl) is in the position of looking up to the man, idolizing him, needing him, being subservient to him (and often *serving* him), and all of this is revealed to him through the fact that she is nearly naked.

Perhaps one of the most classic expressions of this in porn is the Catholic School Girl, who looks so innocent in her tiny plaid uniform skirt, braids, and knee socks, an image famously emulated by Britney Spears in her first video from 1998, "Baby One More Time." Pre-Internet, this four-minute clip not only cemented sixteen-year-old Spears's instant pop-stardom but her corresponding reputation as the real life Virgin-Whore straight out of pornographic fantasy. The video opens with Spears sitting in a Catholic high-school classroom, bored by her teacher, tapping her pencil against her book, and pouting her lips, her long blond hair drawn up in two adorable, little girl braids tied with prim pink bands. When the bell rings, she's up and into the hall. The music starts, and soon she whips off her gray cardigan and is dancing around, her white oxford shirt completely unbuttoned and knotted across her chest, sleeves rolled up, bra showing, midriff bare, her schoolgirl skirt mid-thigh and twirling up suggestively every time she spins, her knee socks suddenly hitting the edge of her thighs like the thigh-high boots often associated with prostitutes in television and movies. There's an entire dance team of similarly dressed schoolgirls backing her up, all of whom are half-naked, decked out to look extra adorable, yet having transformed the traditional Catholic school uniform designed to cover girls up into something so revealing it screams both "I'm sexy" and "I'm innocent." When the boys in the video join in the dancing, they are dressed in conservative Catholic schoolboy uniforms, with blazers on, oxfords buttoned to their necks, and ties perfect. The boys wear long pants with their shirts tucked in; they are fully, properly, and appropriately clothed for school.

The real-life Britney Spears boasted about her sexual innocence—how she was a virgin waiting to have sex until she got married. At least for a couple of years, she became the iconic contradiction in terms: the girl who oozed sex when performing, the portrait of the porn fantasy, yet whose real-life little-girl speaking voice and claims of sexual innocence were of the kind that men (allegedly) dream about. In many ways, this was the oldest male fantasy in the book: the girl who seems as pure as can be but who he imagines will turn out to be shockingly wild in the bedroom.

What completes the fantasy in actual pornography is how a woman (or girl) literally makes herself sexually available to the man (or boy). She presents herself as not only willing, but wanting him. The woman "suggests" this by taking the uniform of whatever submissive role she's in—maid, cheerleader, secretary, schoolgirl—and turning it into an outfit that reveals all. The skirt becomes so short he can see her underwear (or lack thereof). She doesn't button her shirt at all. Her bra is lace, see-through, and visible via her skimpy outfit. A wide swath of midriff is bared. Above all, her "job" is to visually become the ultimate male fantasy. But instead of standing before him as an unreachable pop star or porn star in a video, now she's the girl from his American Lit class and she's standing right in from of him at a college party.

BY THE TIME YOUNG MEN AND WOMEN step foot on campus today, they know all the right sex-speak, how to sext and talk dirty online to each other (often through videos), as well as the intricacies and technicalities of sexual positions and tricks. They have all the trappings of sexually experienced men and women; they might know how to be fantastic sexual performers and talkers, on the surface—adept at pretending. But their emotional maturity with respect to sex is another question altogether. They've been taught that both men and women are supposed to have "sex like a man," that is, to hook up, even if they haven't yet hooked up themselves. They are also growing up to believe that all of this is normal. And that to act like porn stars is normal, too.

So this "new normal": men and women learning about sex through Internet porn and adjusting their expectations for their partners accordingly, is reflected in the trends on college campuses, where students get to live out all of this sexy education on the party circuit. Again, this trend reveals a dissonance between outward and inward reality. Both young men and young women understand the importance of making themselves desirable à la the porn industry, yet at the same time they are becoming ever more distanced from their own desires. Desire has taken a back seat to desirability, and this process has been exacerbated and intensified by everyone's exposure to porn. Women have learned how to sex themselves up like porn stars to go out to parties, while men are well socialized to posture around them in the equivalent, stereotypical male porn-star roles. Consider the following scenarios:

CEOs and Their Secretary Hos

Dirty Doctors and Naughty Nurses

Maids and Millionaires

Gold Pros and Tennis Hos

Professors and Naughty Schoolgirls

Football Players and Cheerleaders

Superheroes and Supersluts

Sex [short for Secretaries] and Execs

Horny Housewives and Randy Handymen

These are the kind of role-play pairings regularly found in porn—but they are also the role-plays typically played out live at college parties today. Every single one of these pairings comes from responses students gave in the online survey for my study. These students weren't answering a question about porn, however; they were describing how they party, calling up the go-to "themes" that determine how men and women are supposed to dress when they go out. Go to any Catholic, private-secular, or public institution of higher education on a given weekend and you will find at least some version of a "Politicians and Prostitutes" or "Santa and his Reindeer Ho, Ho, Hos" party (or insert appropriate holiday theme), and many and varied adaptations of such events. By design, these are parties that cater to extreme, dualistic stereotypes about men, women, and sex and that play around with those classic categories of Good Girl, Prude, and Slut.[1]

The range of scenarios for getting women to show up nearly naked—and trashed, too, since alcohol is an essential aspect of theme parties—is only growing more creative. The titles of the events make it sound as if the college campus turns into a porn set on Friday and Saturday nights, with guys (and sometimes women, too) directing and setting up scenes that will allow them to play out male sexual fantasies. Even if the women throw the parties, their roles remain the subservient ones, with the themes depending on porn scenarios that cater to men. The women who attend these events and dress up for them don't seem to understand how degrading these expectations are either. And theme parties only intensify the pressure that both women and men feel to hook up.

It was in 2004 while teaching an undergraduate class that I first found out about theme parties. My students were discussing images of the divine as they relate to the struggle with and devaluing of the woman's body in Western culture, as well as the feminist argument for breaking down dichotomous hierarchies of God over world, public over private, man over woman, and so on, because these dichotomies disempower women in religious communities and the broader society. My students were considering the contention that "if God is always male, then men become gods,"[2] a phrase that provoked one of my students' hands to go up, at which point she announced, "Men make themselves into gods at parties on the weekend." When I asked her to clarify what she meant, curious to better understand the leap of imagination she'd made from theory to what she saw on campus, she answered simply that men always "play the god role" at what she then called "theme parties."

At this point, other class members began nodding their heads in recognition and shouting out some of the different "themes" from parties they'd attended. I wrote them up on the whiteboard under the rubric of those dichotomous hierarchies we'd been discussing all semester, where God and men sit on the upper left of a horizontal dividing line and human and woman took the lower left spot. I added the "god roles" from theme parties along the top of the line, and their corresponding female roles along the bottom.

GOD / MAN	HUMAN / WOMAN
Rational	Emotional
Public	Private
CEOs	Hos
Office Hos	Secretary Hos
Golf Pros	Tennis Hos
Pimps	Hos
Professors	Schoolgirls
Millionaires	Maids

We were soon looking at a visible structure for the campus party scene where, on any given weekend, all social positions of power, respectability, and success were taken up by men, and where women's only options were basically *whore, whore, whore*, and *whore*—then *schoolgirls* and *maids*. My students went on to discuss how a select group of male students on campus not only determined the when, where, and who of the social scene, but also the how of women's dress, since to attend one of these parties, women had to arrive virtually naked to get in the door.

Learning that even the student party culture on campus placed men into positions of power and codified the notion that women were only allowed to be in roles where they were objectified sexually, and that the students *played it out like porn videos*, was rather sickening. When I asked why women attended these parties, my students explained that theme parties were a dominant part of the social scene. But they also discussed the appeal these parties held for them. Students who regularly attended theme parties argued that they provided the only "legitimate" opportunity for women to dress in revealing or sexy attire. There was a clear desire among many women students to dress in a certain manner that, outside of the "safety" of a themed event, would garner them a permanent reputation as "whore" or "slut." If they agreed to the social contract of theme-party culture and only wore this type of attire at the parties, they got a free pass. They could dress and act like a whore for an evening without the fear of gaining a bad reputation. Before this class discussion, it had not occurred to my students to wonder why men always assigned themselves (or were assigned) all the "god-level" roles, leaving women always and only assigned to the role of whore for the men on campus.

Theme parties have begun to fulfill an interesting, yet profoundly disturbing, function on campuses today. They structure a certain kind of sexual role-playing between men and women within hookup culture, yet one where the themed nature of the function alleviates the participants of feeling responsible for the behavior that occurs in that context. In a way, it is similar to the way alcohol alleviates responsibility. Theme parties provide an oasis of shame-free and guilt-free activity, where students are able to play the roles of pimp and whore as if they were acting in a play. The party itself provides a fiction-like space for this behavior. The parameters of the event dictate that whatever happens at the party can be left behind when one goes home afterward.

As I began to investigate this trend for my study, I learned that "Pimps and Hos" is the "classic" theme party—or at least it's the original. "Pimps and Hos" is where this "tradition" (as some students refer to it) started at the college level, although lately, some students simply call all theme parties "Porn Parties." Other variations that students mentioned include "Lingerie Parties," "Sex-Ed Parties," and "Ho-Downs." There are "Farmer Joes and Tractor Hos" parties, "Santa's Ho Ho Hos" for Christmas, "GI Joe and Jane Ho," or just the basic "Army Ho." The variety of names people have for the more generic "CEOs and Secretary Hos" party is rather startling—from "Businessmen and Office Sluts" to the simpler "CEOs and Corporate Hos," which perhaps gives the woman's role a bit more breadth than the narrower category of "Secretary." Variations on sports themes are extensive as well, with men always in the sports hero / professional / star role and women always as some version of the "Sports Ho."

"We've had just about any kind of male professional / female slut party you can think of," commented one young man in response to a question about theme parties for the online survey. "Pretty much anything and hos," said another. That women are always expected to both play and act the whore is both assumed and accepted as a theme-party norm.

One young woman revealed a paradox in the frustration she felt about how guys get to watch women show up for the parties practically naked and the simultaneous desire she felt to be desirable to those same guys. "I feel like most theme parties are an excuse for girls to dress really trashy (short skirts, boobs coming out of their top, lots of makeup)," she wrote. About the play-acting aspect of these parties, she added, "A lot of the time, any theme costume is turned into hardly wearing any clothing at all. It's like you're not being 'yourself.'" She went on to describe her conflicting emotions about the imbalanced situation that theme parties create for men and women on campus. "I think guys really enjoy theme parties because they can just stand there and watch the girls, and then cross their fingers that maybe some stupid drunk girl will let them take advantage of [her]," she wrote. "Theme parties always seem like it's just for the girls to parade around and let the guys look at them. I used to go to theme parties all the time in high school at a local college campus. . . . I would go to them because my friends were going and it did feel like an excuse to look really trashy and [have] it be 'okay.' I liked the attention that was given to me because of what I was wearing."

Like my students who first brought theme parties to my attention, a lot of women on a range of campuses expressed similar feelings about liking the attention they received at these events. The strong desire among many college women to appear and act sexy was evident, but they did not feel they could safely be sexy just anywhere—they needed theme parties to provide a forum in which they could experiment with the notion of sexiness and live out the new societal expectations of them. The women also believed that by dressing this way they would be able to get the male attention they craved—male attention that has become extremely fraught and difficult to win in any other way within the context of hookup culture.

"I usually walk through once or twice and just stand along the periphery, observing," wrote one young man, who said he regularly attended theme parties but didn't like to think he was part of this scene. "My friends and I usually attend these parties just to watch how stupidly drunk people at them tend to get, especially girls. Girls often get the most drunk at these 'Theme Parties,' which is often the incentive for single guys to attend, in hopes of having sex."

The observation that people drink especially hard at theme parties was common. Alcohol is considered liquid courage, and theme parties only heighten the need to self-medicate. The perception that women drank even more at these events than at other parties revealed some of the alienation they felt from themselves in these situations—in order to sufficiently gear up to attend a party half-naked, they needed even more alcohol than usual.

"If I was single, I would probably not stand on the outside of the party as much," this same young man continued:

Often inside these parties, [there is] a lot of dancing to current hip-hop or old nostalgic songs; basically any songs that keep the girls happy and dancing. The dancing is often a form of clothed vertical humping. At one end of the party is a supply of liquors or some strong concoction. As the party winds on and people have had a lot of booze, the dancing becomes sadly more unrhythmic and distinctly more lascivious. People usually begin to wander off toward rooms or their own places. Those left behind are either drunk to the point of fighting or . . . watching the "too drunk" people.

At theme parties, the pressures to make oneself sexually available, to have a quick, no-strings-attached encounter—or at the very least to collect gossip about who is doing what with whom—are explicitly and visually set up as if on stage, with both men and women performing and play-acting to the best of their abilities. If hookup culture at a basic level is a culture of pretend, then theme parties only exacerbate this, alienating students even further from their own desires and from each other through the roles they are expected to play.

When I describe this scene during lecture visits, faculty members, administrators, and parents are all shocked, not only by the idea of theme parties, but by the way students discuss them and how they dress for them. The adults in students' lives are confused about why anyone—especially a young woman at college—would be willing to subjugate herself to such raunchy expectations. Yet perhaps we shouldn't be all that surprised, given the way these themes are also playing out in the broader culture.

BEFORE TECHNOLOGY MADE PORN as ubiquitous as watching clips on YouTube, it was largely a male consumer industry. It produced movies and magazines that men indulged in when no one else was looking, and they didn't dare tell anybody. Times have changed, and the way both men and women in American culture consume porn has changed as well. Porn is no longer something to hide. What's more, it's a hobby women have lately been socialized to take up with glee.

In her 2005 book *Pornified: How Pornography Is Transforming Our Loves, Our Relationships, and Our Families*, journalist Pamela Paul argued that men are bound by certain societal restrictions: they cannot eye a woman's cleavage in the workplace, they cannot stare at her no matter how tight her jeans, but "in porn, [women treat] a man the way he wants to be treated, relieving him of the fears that plague everyday male-female interaction. In the porn world, men retain the power and the control. It's an incredibly seductive fantasy." She added that porn has become so popular that men's expectations have shifted. They expect women to give in and act like porn stars to please them. What's more, "many men don't even realize that what they're asking for is degrading or unpleasant to women," Paul wrote. The raunchy has become mainstream.[3]

In *Female Chauvinist Pigs*, echoing Paul's arguments, Ariel Levy discussed the rise of "raunch culture," which gets women to buy into and perform well for "guy culture." To illustrate this, Levy followed a "Girls Gone Wild" (GGW) television crew around Miami, as they sought willing female participants to perform for their pornographic videos. Wearing GGW hats and T-shirts, Levy wrote about how the men were constantly approached by girls willing to flash them or strip completely, make out with each other, masturbate on camera, or mime sex acts on each other—all for a piece of GGW paraphernalia. Levy argued that the things feminists used to reject—*Playboy*, pornography, debasement—are now being embraced by young women as reclamations of their sexuality and as empowerment. The current accepted wisdom, she wrote, is that "the only alternative to enjoying *Playboy* (or flashing for *Girls Gone Wild* or getting implants or reading Jenna Jameson's memoir) is being 'uncomfortable' with and 'embarrassed' about your sexuality. Raunch culture, then, isn't an entertainment option, it's a litmus test of female uptightness."[4]

Then in February 2011, *New York Magazine* devoted an entire issue to the way the rise and ease of access to porn on the Internet is changing attitudes about sex and the way boys and girls experience desire. The cover article, "They Know What Boys Want," focuses on how social media and Internet porn are influencing junior-high and high-school girls' understanding of sexiness. Girls are learning to use porn and porn archetypes to impress boys as early as middle school. A separate article in the same issue dealt with how, when boys grow up on porn and grow accustomed to using porn as a regular part of their sex lives, several outcomes are possible. Some boys lose interest in sex—why have sex with another person when you can orgasm from seeing videos all by yourself? But many boys learn to assume that the things women do in porn—how they dress and act around men—is also how women are supposed to act in real life. These same boys are learning to expect girls their own age to act like the women in the porn videos, too.[5]

On top of the rise of Internet porn and the rest of the porn industry, there are other influences in society dedicated to teaching young girls that it's never too early to sex themselves up for the boys. A widespread consumer culture of "sexualization" has been much discussed in newspapers and several recent popular books. The term denotes the way girls are being socialized to become sexpots as early as age seven or eight—the same girls who grow up to be those "liberated women" willing to take it all off for a "Girls Gone Wild" baseball hat or t-shirt, or to dress up as a wide variety of "Hos," maids, and schoolgirls. In "Playing at Sexy," a 2010 article in the *New York Times Magazine*, Peggy Orenstein wrote of the "ongoing confusion between desirability and desire" among tween and teen girls, and how many girls have no idea how to connect the "sexy attitudes" they learn to affect with "erotic feeling." Girls learn very young how to be desirable—to *look* hot, to *dance* sexy, to *talk* dirty. It's easy for a girl to know how to act sexy, but to feel sexy, to desire sex, is something most of these same "sexy girls" have never experienced, Orenstein observed.[6]

In *The Triple Bind: Saving Our Teenage Girls from Today's Pressures*, Stephen Hinshaw and Rachel Kranz argued that the sexualization and oversexualization of children and teenagers stems from pop culture marketed toward them. Between the sexy images sold to girls, as well as the constant encouragement to be sexy themselves, girls learn to dress slutty, dance like strippers, and use their sexiness to wield power over boys. And all this happens long before they're emotionally mature enough to even understand their sexiness, let alone their feelings toward boys and relationships. Hinshaw and Kranz culled recent mainstream media articles to compile an alarming list of products sold and marketed toward very young girls in the past few years that perpetuate the sexualization of girlhood: "In 2003," they wrote, "$1.6 million worth of thong underwear was bought for girls ages seven to twelve to wear." In addition, "toy manufacturers are selling black leather miniskirts for girls under eight. A televised Victoria's Secret fashion show featured seven- to nine-year-olds modeling sexy underwear. Abercrombie and Fitch sells girls'-size T-shirts with slogans like 'Who needs brains when you've got these?' And girls in the six-to-twelve 'tween' market are being targeted by the makers of Bratz dolls, whose outfits include halter tops and faux-fur armlets. . . . There's even a new term for overly sexualized youngsters: *prosti-tots*." In a culture where a term like "prosti-tots" is necessary to characterize how young girls are being socialized to grow up, perhaps it's not so surprising that these same girls are expected to graduate to the role of porn star on the party scene when they go off to college.[7]

This topic is also intelligently discussed in *Packaging Girlhood: Rescuing Our Daughters from Marketer's Schemes*, in which psychologists Sharon Lamb and Lyn Mikel Brown devote their discussion to the industries and moneymaking juggernauts that have sprung up around this marketer's mission. Much like Hinshaw and Kranz, Lamb and Brown examine how marketers have co-opted the term "girl power" and translated it into a tool to convince a girl "that she is independent and making her own choices, making her *believe* she is free by selling her an *image* of a free girl." At the same time they are selling her a Halloween costume that has her nearly naked as she steps out into the freezing night. And that's when she is only ten.

The gender divide in children's Halloween costumes is alarming. "Little girls don't 'take on evil' or have 'bold adventures' or even 'incredible fun,'" Lamb and Brown wrote. "They don't save, capture, leap, strike fear, or stop enemies—they don't *do anything*. . . . When we checked a promisingly neutral 'When I Grow Up' category on one [Halloween] site[,] . . . parents [could] find fifty-five costumes for boys and only twenty-two for girls. Of these, fifteen [were] cheerleaders, divas, and rock stars. Included in this 'when I grow up' section was our number one thumbs-down nomination. Don't all parents wish their daughter will grow up to be a 'French maid'?"

What is most interesting about Lamb and Brown's discussion of gender and Halloween, for our purposes, is that Halloween is the holiday that many college students cite as the original example of what they call theme-party culture. This is where it all began. And most men and women on campus have come to view Halloween as an all-purpose theme party, assuming that every girl that goes out on this night will dress trashy in the guise of some sort of costume. The theme party itself is only Halloween extended into every other time of year.[8]

As Ariel Levy and researchers such as Lamb and Brown have shown, the sexualization of women through consumer and raunch culture is certainly not what feminism was supposed to be about. Theme parties and excessive alcohol consumption, and every other activity in which student agency and autonomy take a back seat to fitting in, celebrate all that hookup culture brings to the social scene. Students want to fit in, even at the expense of everything they believe in about how others should be treated and how they would like to be treated themselves.

The fact that theme parties like this occur on college campuses at all should seem strange, given that these are institutions where young women and young men supposedly go to develop critical-thinking skills. The sexualized ways in which they socialize, dress, and act betray a disconnect between their classroom selves and their personal lives—the exact kind of disconnect I spoke about at the beginning of this book. In the classroom, students are perfectly capable of assessing and evaluating ideas; meanwhile, they let their lives go unexamined. They not only allow others to devalue them, body and soul, but they do the same to others and to themselves.

It's not as though the tools for assessing the truth about theme parties were unavailable to students on campus. But there is not usually an express effort by faculty, administrators, or staff to help students think these things through. When encouraged to put those daytime tools to work to assess their nighttime behaviors, students are well able to understand why it is they do what they do, what it is they have bought into, and how they might step back from it. And that is true not only for the college women, but also for the college men.

Chapter Five

Why We Get Boys Wrong:
The Emotional Glass Ceiling

*It's definitely guys lying to say they've done it more,
and girls lying to say they've done it less.*

—SOPHOMORE WOMAN AT A CATHOLIC COLLEGE

THE NEWS CYCLE LOVES SCANDAL; it loves sex scandal even more. Throw a bunch of teenage boys into the mix, and the public flocks to the debate.

The public certainly pounced on the Milton Academy high-school oral-sex scandal in Boston in 2004–2005 (one girl, five guys on the hockey team, five blow jobs, and five resulting expulsions). It pounced again on the all-boys Landon School's "fantasy football" scandal in 2010 (the boys had assigned a point system to rate the girls they invited to a party; they planned to have as much sex as possible to rack up points and "win the game").[1]

The ideal set of circumstances for provoking controversy throws in questions about how we are raising our children today, and what, indeed, this world is coming to, if this is how our boys are indulging themselves. Often, the worried and the shocked express their concern against a backdrop of other folks who are rather gleefully "heh, heh, hehing" about how boys will be boys, and there is nothing we can do about it.

With regard to attitudes about sex, men get a bad rap, especially the young ones, and the films that celebrate raunchy guys behaving badly go all the way back to *Animal House*. More recent are Judd Apatow's wildly popular movies, including *The 40-Year-Old Virgin* and *Knocked Up*, which present an in-between boy-man who is crass about women and sex (the same kind of guy who drives women to hook up, according to Hanna Rosin). But somewhere in this boy-man's brain and body lies a heart of gold. After the cast of male characters spends the better part of two hours spewing vulgarities, and the scenarios involving comedic sex or sex-avoidance play out, this heart of gold is somehow revealed.[2] Apatow has been lauded for portraying men who are *ultimately* sensitive to and respectful of women—who, deep down, want committed relationships—yet more than anything else, his movies celebrate the notion that boys don't ever really have to learn to be men.

Somehow his audience allows itself to be shepherded to this epiphany by a whole lot of "boys will be boys" antics and a level of crudeness about women that led even Katherine Heigl, the actress who starred in *Knocked Up*, to rather famously comment, in *Vanity Fair*, that she felt uncomfortable with the fact that the movie was "a little sexist." "[*Knocked*

Up] paints the women as shrews, as humorless and uptight, and it paints the men as lovable, goofy, fun-loving guys," she said. "It exaggerated the characters, and I had a hard time with it, on some days. I'm playing such a bitch; why is she being such a killjoy? Why is this how you're portraying women? Ninety-eight percent of the time it was an amazing experience, but it was hard for me to love the movie."[3] Yet moviegoers seemed perfectly fine with this paradox, and not at all worried about the messages it sent about what it meant to be a woman or a man in American culture.

The stereotype that men are animals and will act like animals until a woman civilizes them is not only exploited in popular culture and the broader media. It's also the kind of rigid view of gender common to evangelical books that give advice about dating, purity, courtship, and marriage to teens and young adults. Much of this literature teaches young men that they are naturally sexual predators. One guide by a Christian author tells young men that the "ultimate test of your manhood" is to "1) Think clearly 2) About sex." The presumption is that, when it comes to sex, men's brains stop working, and all sorts of idiotic, unfeeling, hurtful, and jerkish behavior ensues— and that men can't help this.[4] In the most successful manual in this genre, *Every Young Man's Battle: Strategies for Victory in the Real World of Sexual Temptation*, authors Stephen Arterburn and Fred Stoeker employ war metaphors in their discussions of men and sex, speaking of all men as sex addicts who need to be taught how to cope with their "addictive sexual cravings."[5]

For a young man not to feel such constant lust for women the second they hit puberty is the equivalent to failing in one's masculinity.

From all directions, young men are taught that they want sex far more than young women do, and that part of their job— part of what it means to be a man—is to either continually battle to deny themselves any indulgence in sex (the Christian view) or to trick women into having sex, even if this requires lying to them (the secular view). What we don't see much in our culture is an intelligent gender critique for men, by men, on the movie, TV, sex, and porn industries.

The kind of critiques we do see—like those of Ariel Levy, Sharon Lamb, and Lyn Mikel Brown—are often maligned by those who are made nervous by the authors' feminist stand- points. The running joke among gender studies professors about why so few men sign up for courses in this field is that, although women know they are gendered, men haven't yet realized this about themselves. Our culture tends to deny, or at least dis- courage, men and boys from thinking extensively, critically, and in a group of their peers about why they are the way they are, what makes a guy a "guy," and whether being a "guy" is something to which they truly aspire.

This unfortunate deficiency only perpetuates societal ac- ceptance of the idea that girls are naturally the "sexual objects," and that boys are there to objectify them. Formal discussions, gossip, and the college party scene orbit around this basic in- terpretation of the way things are, too, but there is very little, if any, worry about the sexualization of boys into "guys," who are understood as wanting nothing more than getting into girls' pants. For decades, most of our public attention and discussion of sexualization and the pressures society exerts about sexuality have centered disproportionately on women and girls. Though Lamb and Brown followed up *Packaging Girlhood* with a companion book, *Packaging Boyhood: Saving Our Sons from Superheroes, Slackers, and Other Media Stereotypes*, there is little else on the market covering this topic. A man has yet to get around to publishing something akin to *The Masculine Mystique* that will speak to a generation of boys and men who know deep down that something isn't quite right about manhood in America culture.

With the media and popular culture trumpeting these "boys will be boys" stereotypes far and wide, we get a view of boys in relation to sex that is egregious, at best. Perhaps it isn't so surprising, then, when some of these boys start acting scandalously in real life, as the boys involved in the "fantasy football" scandal at Landon School did. Hookup culture mirrors this model, with the job of the guy being to treat the girl like trash, and the job of the "ho" to become the trash ready to be thrown out. And all of this also goes a long way toward explaining why so many college students, young men and women alike, feel perfectly comfortable living out a paradox of playful degradation at theme parties. This is how culture tells them they are *supposed* to act.

If societal stereotypes of men and masculinity were largely true, then hookup culture on college campuses would seem like a male Promised Land. Most people imagine that the traits of hooking up—quick, casual sexual encounters with someone you just met that take place just down the hall in your buddy's room for twenty minutes, leaving you free to go back to join the party without skipping a beat—are male by design.

But what if they aren't? What if we keep getting the reality of today's boys wrong? What if we are raising boys to play the game, so to speak, even at the cost of what they really want? What if, just like young women, young men have become such good actors and performers on the social stage that they can't find their way back to anything that is real? And while stereotypes may rather accurately portray the kind of behavior that our society *expects* from its boys, what if these approximations don't reflect what boys actually wish they could expect from themselves?

THE SOCIOLOGIST MICHAEL KIMMEL'S *Guyland: The Perilous World Where Boys Become Men* is a rare critical reflection on guy culture in America. Kimmel looked at Western ideas and constructions of masculinity and manhood in a critique similar to the one feminist scholars have been engaging about women and girlhood for decades, and many of his views about men and guy culture resonate with my findings about young men in hookup culture. Kimmel talks of "Guyland" as a culture of pretend, where "acting like a guy" is a learned skill that has little to do with how a man really feels about women, sex, and relationships. Guyland is, most of all, a proving ground for

masculinity among male peers that most young men are throw.
into, like it or not. Guyland leaves young men forced to act
like someone they are not.

"In an effort to prove their masculinity, with little guidance
and no real understanding of what manhood is, [guys] engage
in behaviors that are ill-conceived and irresponsibly carried
out," Kimmel wrote. "These are guys so desperate to be accepted
by their peers that they do all sorts of things they secretly know
to be not quite right. They lie about their sexual experiences
to seem more manly; they drink more than they know they
can handle because they don't want to seem weak or immature;
they sheepishly engage in locker-room talk about young women
they actually like and respect."[6]

Kimmel returned to these points throughout *Guyland*, but
this was also where his research became strange. He asserted
that guys were not really into this awful, vulgar, and sometimes
hateful behavior and commentary; yet throughout *Guyland*,
his portraits of "real guys" only reinforce stereotypical notions
about college men. Despite Kimmel's belief that the larger culture of "Guyland" is the culprit, *Guyland* is highly populated
by jerks and rarely by young men who bemoan their conscrip-
tion into the culture. Kimmel offered only a single chapter—
at the end of *Guyland*, called "Just Guys"—to show anything
that goes against the stereotype. The chapter reveals a number
of young men who support his initial argument—that guys
really aren't so bad after all. Perhaps this contradiction in *Guyland* is rooted in the fact that Kimmel spoke to men almost

exclusively in peer groups—he caught them hanging out watching television, playing video games, and in precisely the kind of scenarios where I learned that college men do the most posturing: in front of each other.

Kimmel is absolutely right that young men in America are socialized to lie, to boast, and to remain silent about their emotions. In my experience, the only way to get the story about how college men really feel is to give them a private space in which to discuss or write about what they are thinking. In this safe space, they do not have to worry about the opinions of the other "guys" around them. If part of the problem is that young men have learned to posture and perform for each other, then we cannot expect them to suddenly drop the pretend game for a focus group.

Some statistics from recent studies do show that men like hookup culture more than women do, or at least they say they do. In one such investigation, 26 percent of women reported a positive reaction after hooking up, 49 percent reported a negative one, and 25 percent said they were ambivalent, whereas 50 percent of the male respondents reported a positive reaction, 26 percent reported a negative one, and 23.6 percent were ambivalent. Yet even this data does not paint a picture of your average college guy loving hookup culture; about half of the above men surveyed were either negative or ambivalent, at best, about their hookups.[7]

The portrait of college men as having lots of sex and not caring about what they did the night before is common, but finding that stereotypical college guy is more difficult than one might think. I did encounter a few in my interviews. All of them were strikingly similar: good-looking, charismatic, popular, a number of them athletes. The most significant characteristic tying them all together, though, was not a veneer of "guyness," but the fact that their "guyness" went all the way through to their cores. These were the young men who didn't feel unease with guy culture. Instead, they celebrated it and reveled in it. These men lived up to the stereotypes about guys, and, sadly, also seemed to be the people on campus who set the standard for masculinity. So even though true guys' guys were rare, the average man on campus understands that if he wants to see social success as a male, he had better act like these alpha males. Reinforcing this standard are the women on campus who throw themselves at these "true guys."[8]

In my interviews and conversations with men, it seemed that hookup culture did not so much cater to heterosexual men and male desire as it did to male anxieties about living up to so much sexual expectation. And although the culture certainly gets in the way of women's happiness, one of the most obvious differences in the comments made by men and women during the interviews had to do with the fact that, while women felt (mostly) free to complain out loud about how much they disliked hookup culture and its corresponding pressures, men felt they were not allowed this same freedom. Men are required to grin and bear hookup culture without expressing dissent, even if they, too, hope for more from their encounters and feel disappointed with the lack of meaning in their relationships. Whereas women risk gaining a lasting reputation as a slut by participating in hookup culture, men risk gaining a reputation by *not* being a part of it.

"The first semester I hooked up with a few different people, and in the moment it's great, and that is really what you are looking for," explained a first-year man at a Catholic college. "But if you are looking for a relationship, [the hookup] is a cheap substitute for it. Then the next day there is usually some guilt tied to it. It's fun because you think you are going somewhere and then the next day you realize it's nothing."

For many of the men I interviewed, the anti-emotionality of hooking up is supposed to facilitate racking up lots of sexual conquests. This is what guys know and will say in public. But in private, they often expressed reasons for being a part of hookup culture that had little to do with easy access to experiences of sexual gratification. "A lot of people do think that for guys to be promiscuous is cool," said another first-year student at a Catholic school, who felt frustrated by this pressure. "Personally, I don't think it's cool." A young man at one of the secular universities said, simply, "To reject someone because you aren't interested in a hookup isn't acceptable."

Another young man, also from a secular school, spoke extensively on the relationship between hookup culture and the party scene. He explained that guys don't have to participate in all of it, but the consequence of such a decision is ending up alone. "If you don't want to have any pressure, it's very easy . . . to disappear," he began. "But that also leads to people being depressed. Like, why are you not hanging out? Sometimes a little pressure is good, like [your friends saying], 'No, come out, come out!' . . . But if no one's going to drag you out, then you might get . . . I don't know, *sad*." According to this student, being a part of hookup culture is about camaraderie. Getting "dragged" into it is part of how you avoid feeling lonely and sad, even though many students say that hookup culture is also the *source* of their loneliness.

Many of the women I interviewed had strong opinions of "guy culture" on campus and spoke of how a large part of what it means to be a "guy" is to have lots of meaningless sex for the express purpose of being able to boast about it to your friends later. "I think with guys, [hooking up] always goes with a sort of machoness that you are expected to uphold," said one young woman from a Catholic school. "I think sexuality and sexual experiences go hand in hand with machoness, especially at this age. The more experiences you have, the cooler you are. With a guy anyway." Another young woman at a secular university said, "I feel like it's celebrated in the male community for getting with however many girls." This was a common refrain from women across Catholic and secular institutions. To establish your masculinity on campus as a guy is to establish yourself as a frequent partaker of hookup culture, engaging in whatever behavior it takes to prove this.

Hooking up is a numbers game for college men. The more hookups a guy can claim, the better off he will be in the eyes of other guys, and the more "guy-like" he will seem. The more vulgar a guy's talk about his hookups (including the ones he makes up), the more credible he is as a guy. Even if someone does not like hooking up that much, even if he feels ambivalent about hookup sex, and even if what he really wants is a long-term relationship, hookup culture requires him to act like a boy-man who is vulgar on the outside and maybe, *maybe*, in a Judd-Apatow-movie way, civilizable eventually. Hookup culture frowns on men for publicly expressing their feelings, showing vulnerability, and being openly emotional. Such traits are associated with weakness and the erosion of masculinity, with many young men living in fear of this occurring to them. So men posture, perform, and posture some more.

When young men are provided anonymity to speak, many reveal that hookup culture fosters sexual performance anxiety. Some evaluated hookups not by whether they and their partners enjoyed the experience, but by how they believed their guy friends would judge the woman with whom they hooked up. In the online survey, one first-year man referred to both the worth of his female partner and his sexual performance during the hookup, the sexual performance piece being the more important marker of success. "I thought she was a fun girl," he wrote, "and I thought I was pretty great." But a number of respondents evaluated their hookups according to whether the girl was pretty or not—specifically, whether they thought their guy friends would evaluate the girls as hot or not.

If a young man believed his friends would give his partner a pass as far as looks went, then he could feel good about the hookup; if he believed that other men would deem her unattractive, then he knew to feel embarrassed or even ashamed about hooking up with her. One senior cataloged his feelings about hooking up in relation to his partner. "If she's attractive and there's evidence that I used protection, I feel extremely positive about my actions," he began. "If she decides to hang out too long, wanting breakfast or cuddle time, this begins to make me angry and I feel less positive. If she is not good looking and/or [is] friends or acquaintances with someone who knows I have a girlfriend, I regret my actions and wish I had shown more self-control the night before."

More common even than these "it depends on the girl's looks" responses were those exclusively about sexual performance anxiety. Whether or not a male student felt okay about a hookup experience depended upon whether he believed the woman enjoyed it. Many men expressed fear that the girl didn't enjoy herself, yet they were also too embarrassed to ask her if she did. Since a hookup is about *not* communicating, many men were left worried that there were women wandering around on campus who thought they were awful in bed. A bad performance in bed puts men at risk of negative gossip and a bad reputation. Whether most of the young men were more worried about negative gossip or about the partner herself having a good sexual experience for her own benefit wasn't clear.

But for some men, the whole experience of hooking up was simply awful on every level.

"Sometimes I don't remember what happened [in a hookup] due to intoxication," recounted one young man, a first-year student. "And when I wake up next to someone, I think it was a really dumb decision, get up and leave the room hoping that they will leave before I return. I usually take a shower to rid myself mentally and physically [and] never want it to happen again." Like so many women, many men find it difficult to face their partners sober the next morning.

Another young man, a senior, spoke not only about regretting hookups, but about how hooking up made him feel taken advantage of. This is an experience people tend to associate with women, not men, because many people can't imagine a man who wouldn't want to engage in sex every time the opportunity arose. "I often feel as though I've betrayed myself and my values by being physically intimate with someone I do not share an emotional intimacy with," this young man wrote in the online survey. "I sometimes feel as though my partner has taken advantage of me, even if I first approached her. I feel my actions arise more from a desire to please my partner and a desire not to spend the night alone more than anything else, and I look at hooking up, and how I look at hooking up, as signs of my own insecurity."

Out of 164 college men who wrote short essays about their hookup experiences, 63 of them (39 percent) expressed extreme regret, shame, and frustration with themselves about it. They spoke of feeling stupid because they'd hooked up, how it was an awkward experience, and how it made them feel "bad" and often "guilty" or "insecure." The largest group of men who talked about hooking up expressed a lot of ambivalence about this activity—these were young men who claimed that hooking up made them feel "nothing" or "the same" (it didn't matter much to them if they hooked up or not—they could take it or leave it), or "up and down." A few implied they were "comfortable" with hooking up, though not overly excited about the practice. The men who felt rather "blah" about hooking up amounted to 73 out of the 164 respondents (45 percent)—almost half. These were the young men who referred to hookups the way they might refer to eating a bowl of cereal every morning—it was just part of the routine, something they had been taught to believe that "guys" were supposed to do to fit into the college experience.

The satisfaction of male sexual desire or even its presence during hookup sex was largely absent when men reported on their behavior. They talked about sex as if it were boring and as if they were bored by having it. A few men were truly boastful about their conquests, and excited to give details about these experiences, complete with the bravado and vulgarity American culture socializes everyone to expect from college guys. But only 25 men (15 percent) spoke of their hookups in these stereotypical ways, and most of these responses were rather short. One young man, for example, said, "I feel great," without further comment. Another said hooking up made him feel "exultant, proud, calm, satisfied."

When I set out to talk to college students about sex, romance, and hookup culture on campus, I held a lot of my
own preconceived notions about the types of answers I would
get from men. I, too, imagined that, while women would likely
express dissent about hookup culture (which they did), men
would express how much they loved hooking up. I thought
the answers I received from men saying hookups made them
"feel great" or "exultant, proud, calm, [and] satisfied" would
make up the majority of the male responses. But as young
man after young man showed up for their interviews, and as
I began to look over the survey and journal data I gathered,
I found that many men were just as stressed out by hookup
culture as the women. This discovery surprised me. There are
many men out there at colleges and universities across America
who are sad, ashamed, and/or ambivalent about hooking up
and the sex they are having; who wish for long-term relationships, dating, love, and romance; and who feel that their sex
lives are actually pretty unfulfilling, even bad and embarrassing.
If they want to be regarded as "real men" or "guys," however,
they also feel they must go along with hookup culture without
complaint.

In economies where sexual favors are exchanged for a certain
form of social capital, which in the case of hookup culture
tends to be social status (bragging rights for guys, and gossip
and the potential for social elevation and a boyfriend for girls),
we assume that a gender hierarchy exists: that men operate on
the upper levels, holding all the cards, with the authority to

run the game, collect the money, and make the important decisions, and that women are relegated to the bottom, with little or no say in what goes on, forced to submit to whatever rules men draw up. Hookup culture, at first glance, and with its preponderance of theme parties that exacerbate this gender hierarchy, is one that supports this assumption. It is aimed at a stereotypically male construction of pleasure and women's subservience that supports the possibility of a man having many female sexual partners without having to care about the women emotionally or having to put any effort at all into getting sex. But who stands to benefit the most from this arrangement? It might seem to be the men, because, after all, hookup culture hands them the power and authority to set the rules, and they supposedly desire the outcomes that hookup culture provides. In reality, however, this answer is a bit shaky. Below the surface, the benefits are not so clear for the men, either.

Men do indeed know how to brag to their friends about how great the sex is on campus, and how great the theme parties were where women showed up dressed in whatever "whore" image the boys had dreamed up this time. And the men do engage in no-strings-attached hookups whenever they have the chance. But for a man to complain about hookup culture, to express that what he really wants is romance and candlelit dinners, to know and be known, or to say that he wants to be in love when he has sex—is to risk his masculinity entirely, and any hope of a normal social life with it. Almost universally, guys remain silent because of this, even when they are deeply, profoundly wounded.

In all of my research and visits to campuses in the past several years, I have found that men are the most talented actors of all within hookup culture. They have been taught to appear sex-crazed and reckless, even if what they really feel is something else. The idea fostered in American culture that young men are hypersexual is largely false, and therefore a destructive stereotype to maintain. It not only perpetuates hookup culture on campus but also stunts the ability of young men to grow emotionally. It teaches them to silence their real feelings and desires, which also keeps them from finding fulfilling romantic relationships. Men lose so much from these cultural misperceptions, maybe even more than women do, because at least women are allowed to speak about these feelings without having to worry about putting their femininity at risk.

Our view of men and masculinity in American culture is not only deeply flawed and misleading but disastrous for the psyches of young men. It interferes with their ability to mature and develop emotionally as well as to express emotion, to have healthy and fulfilling relationships and sex lives, to communicate emotional pain when they experience it, to feel empathy, and to do all these things without believing that by doing so, they are imperiling their standing as men. Women experience glass ceilings just about every which way they try to move, but men face an emotional glass ceiling. We ask that they repress their feelings surrounding their own vulnerabilities and need for love, respect, and relationship so intensely that we've convinced them that to express such feeling is to have somehow failed as men; that to express such feeling not only makes them look bad in front of other men, but in front of women, too. And we do all of this on college campuses, where we imagine that students will open up and grow into who they really are. Within hookup culture, no one really wins, but perhaps men lose most of all.

Chapter Six

The Virginity Excuse and Other Modes for Opting Out of Hookup Culture (Sort of)

It's a boost to your ego to take somebody's virginity.
—SOPHOMORE MAN AT A SECULAR UNIVERSITY

I think a lot of my friends had had sex, and I was like, well, I don't want to be the only one. So I just won't talk about it. If they bring it up, I'll make up something.
—JUNIOR WOMAN AT A SECULAR UNIVERSITY

I think vaginal intercourse is when you've lost your virginity. I don't think oral sex takes away your virginity, or anal sex, or kissing. Even if you're naked together in bed I don't think that takes away your virginity.
—FIRST-YEAR STUDENT AT AN EVANGELICAL COLLEGE

WHEN COLLEGE STUDENTS ARE confronted by the word "virginity," it registers on a personal level. They belong to one camp or the other—the virgins or the non-virgins—and they catalog their peers and themselves according to these categories. To be a virgin within the context of hookup culture can feel akin to wearing a scarlet letter while crossing the quad. But it can also function as something else, a boundary a student may cling to that they will not be expected to cross during a hookup. These labels provide a dividing line of sorts on campus, and students spend a good deal of time pondering their status over and against their friends, wondering whether they are the last remaining virgin among the regular hookup practitioners, or about why their best friend is holding out for what seems like forever. For some students, these thoughts pass fleetingly and without much care, but for others, the topic of virginity can provoke a spark of happiness; a feeling of smugness, relief, or sheer surprise; or, for more than a few, a sickening note of guilt or shame.

Virginity can function as an idea, a state of mind, a kind of ontological status adopted with regard to sexuality; it is a shift often understood as extremely significant, especially if a person is religious. College students see virginity as a characteristic of being, much like blondness or singleness, as something they can change, though most believe that there is no changing back once it's "gone." Their language about virginity involves words like "lose," "give," "steal," "buy," and "win," all of which present virginity as if it were an object a person might misplace, like a penny, or something that could be stolen before a person was aware it had happened. It is a value, a mark, a goal, an excuse, an escape, a prize; something to hang onto, to hide, get rid of, or define and redefine; a source of pride, joy, shame, ambivalence, frustration, anger, and hope. It is given up and then reclaimed; it seems permanent for some and becomes a temporary state for others. Most college students have either recently lost their virginity or, if they haven't, think a lot about when, how, and with whom this will eventually happen.

Navigating virginity on campus is complicated on many levels, especially with respect to gender. Some students are awash with anger about the unfair emphasis placed on a young woman's virginity, despite the expectations of hookup culture and the reality that male peers are routinely high-fived for sleeping around. In the wake of the women's movement and sexual revolution, defining virginity as a single act of penetration of a woman by a man begs consideration of whether such an idea still makes any sense. Within religions, virginity is still defined as a single experience of vaginal intercourse, as something a woman *gives* to a man and that a man *takes* from a woman, a heterosexual act that is divinely ordained and appropriate only within the confines of marriage—a concept that was wholly absent when students at Catholic and secular institutions spoke about what they believed their peers thought about sex on campus. Ideas about virginity in culture and on college campuses have also become complicated by assumptions and biases about sexual orientation. Narrow heterosexual definitions of virginity assume, among other things, that lifelong lesbians and gay men are virgins, but they do so during a time when the LGBTQ community is politically strong, gay marriage is on the rise, and kids are coming out earlier and earlier as stigmas about sexual orientation grow weaker with each new generation.

The Clinton era saw the beginning of a shift in the cultural conversation about the technicalities of sex; the public's fascination with what counts as *real* sex, and what it means to lose one's virginity, technically, increased in this moment as well.[1] The more recent American political and cultural debates about virginity, and the way it is mocked on television shows and in movies, have begun to seem either irrelevant or cruel in the face of living, breathing young adults who are negotiating their sexual identities, decisions, and practices in relation to their personal and their peers' ideas about virginity and what counts as sex.

Despite so much confusion about what virginity is and what it means to lose it, teens and young adults care deeply about how it is defined and who they are in relation to it, both for their social status and for their gender identities—how they understand themselves as a boy or a girl, a young man or a young woman, gay, straight, lesbian, bisexual, queer, or questioning. Virginity affects every single decision young adults make in their emerging sex lives. Regardless of whether a student is politically liberal, conservative, or moderate; religiously devout, spiritually inclined, or atheist—or none of the above—most have an opinion about this concept and its value (or nonvalue) with respect to their identity, self-esteem, sexual history, and significant relationships.

Virginity is important because it provides a boundary by which young men and women learn to navigate sexual experiences and knowledge. Their understanding of this boundary may determine what behaviors they are willing to engage in (or not). It gives them a sense of their relationship to the sexual bodies that they are. It influences the way they speak about themselves in the midst of hookup culture; the way they speak about sex to one another, what they include in these conversations, and what they omit. It influences conversations about sexual orientation, the many types of sex that are possible, and the many ways that bodies work. Virginity is inextricably tied to a student's most intimate ideas about the self. The concept can help students negotiate and reflect on what sex means to them in a broader sense, occasionally getting them to a place where they contemplate that all-important question that few students realize they have the right to ask: what is good sex, according to them, and in what circumstances do they desire to experience it? In what circumstances would having sex make them feel good, as opposed to merely socially included?

We owe these young adults a serious consideration of the role virginity holds as one of the most salient symbols, laws, boundaries, and ideals that culture and religion have given them to negotiate the complexities of their sexual world, one that is now delineated by the rules of hookup culture.

"I THINK IT'S MORE OF A STATE OF MIND," said Jason, a sophomore at a secular university, about how he understood the concept of virginity. Jason was both a virgin and a Christian amid a sea of non-virgins and non-Christians, a reality that left him fairly lonely. But his peers were more powerful than God in defining his view of sex, virginity, and the significance of being a guy who was also a virgin at college.

"Virginity is a very subjective thing," he observed. "People can now *not* count certain sexual encounters because they weren't fun or weren't rewarding." His peers could be rather arbitrary about what they counted as sex. For example, if they didn't like their experience of first-time sex, they could pretend like it didn't happen and still count themselves virgins. He didn't apply this flexibility to his own sexual history, however, and spoke about how he'd engaged in oral sex twice and hooked up on a number of occasions. "From my experience hooking up," he began, "it was a very emotional experience and . . . I immediately recognized its power. I thought that if this is step one, what happens when you go all the way? I immediately realized that sex was something that I was not prepared for. So I made the decision to put it off until I'm older, [though] I didn't really make any of the decisions about anything in between sex and kissing. It was just [heterosexual intercourse] sex I put off."

Through a kind of trial-and-error period of participating in hookup culture, Jason eventually learned what was important to him about sex and opted out of heterosexual intercourse as a way of hanging onto the right to continue to call himself a virgin. Yet this decision also made him feel isolated from his peers, whom he considered very sexually active. He did not tell them about his decision. He was in no hurry to lose his virgin status, yet he still felt enormous pressure to participate in hookup culture.

In my interviews, I found differences in male and female perceptions about a person's status as virgin. For many college men, the stress of "getting over with" being a virgin or "getting rid of" it tended to be more pronounced than with women. Men usually knew to be mortified if they were still virgins during college and to keep this information close. Being a virgin was often regarded as a wall or barrier of sorts between a man and social happiness and acceptability during college. Women, too, tended to regard men who were still virgins during college as strange, and for one woman in particular from a Catholic campus, it was one thing for a girl to be a virgin during college, but another whole level of shame was involved with being a guy and a virgin, even during his first year.

"I don't know if there's a single guy that I know is a virgin on campus that I'm friends with," she said. "No, I take that back—there's *one* that I can think of. I'm friends with a lot of males on campus so it sticks out—*wow*, out of all these people that I know, maybe fifty-plus, there's only this one person that's a virgin. It just seems like being sexually active is the norm at this point in our lives."

What virginity means when oral sex has become the new making out is not only a question for students and young adults, but for the wider public as well.[2] The concern among parents and journalists about epidemics of oral sex correspond with the fascination of late among scholars and reporters with the way adolescents discuss the notion of "technical virginity." In one large-scale study of this subject, approximately 71 percent of the adolescents surveyed considered themselves virgins even after having oral sex, and 16 percent considered themselves virgins after anal sex. Most of the student participants in this study, like the majority of the participants in my study, defined loss of virginity as vaginal intercourse. Other sociologists have found that among fifteen-to nineteen-year-olds, the motivation to remain a "technical virgin" is less about religion and morality than about the fear of pregnancy or STIs. Another major study on "technical virginity" showed that 54 percent of adolescent females and 52 percent of males had engaged in oral sex, but the behavior was much more common among those who had also had vaginal sex. This finding suggests that remaining a "technical virgin" is not a motivating factor when it comes to preferring oral sex over vaginal sex.[3]

Yet for many students I interviewed, especially young women like Maggie and Susan (introduced in Chapter 3), not counting oral sex as an activity that requires a person to forfeit their virgin status becomes the means to participate in hookup culture quite explicitly while still holding something back, a right they felt was extremely important. To outsiders, this sort of line-drawing might seem irrational, laughable, or simply false (in other words, these students are lying to themselves, and really, all types of sex count toward "losing" one's virginity). Yet, when viewed in light of hookup culture and the pressure students feel to at least appear sexually active, this idea becomes easier to understand.

It solves a problem for students, enabling them to participate while allowing them to keep their virgin status, at least in their own minds and the minds of their peers. Oral sex, as one student put it, could help to "make you feel okay, because you did something, but you didn't do *everything*." If such students can prove at least some sexual experience, and demonstrate a casual attitude about it, then their peers might stop pressuring them to "just get on with it" and lose their virginity.

Not a single student at the Catholic, private-secular, and public institutions where I conducted my research said that their peers valued saving heterosexual intercourse for marriage, and only a handful actually said that their close friends (as opposed to their larger peer group) valued saving the same for love. It was incredibly difficult for students to imagine that all knowledge of sexual experience was supposed to transpire over the course of one evening, and students who identified with a particular religious tradition struggled mightily with what they saw as this very antiquated notion of "saving sex for marriage." A wedding night *used* to represent the beginnings of one's sexual education, they thought, but this was back when pornography was not readily available, sexually explicit dialogue and reading material were rare, conversations about the how-to's of sex were taboo, and hookup culture, as students live it today, did not exist. For most students, religion seemed to serve primarily as a provider of guilt, as opposed to a meaningful force that would help them with sexual decision-making. Unless students grew up as evangelical Christians or considered themselves orthodox

in their tradition, religious teachings about sex were fairly meaningless to them.

One young woman I interviewed who identified as Catholic
said she felt that all types of sex were bad sex *for God* (though
not for her), unless these encounters occurred within marriage.
"In today's world, I think it's hard to live up to the teaching,"
she said. "In my case, I know I shouldn't have sex until I'm
married. . . . I know I shouldn't be doing this, but I do it anyway because I get into a situation where I feel like it's the right
thing to do." Even if she felt good about a particular sexual encounter, sooner or later the guilt would show up. "You can
have this great experience with someone, but then, because
you're not in a marriage, it feels like you did something wrong,"
she said. "Not because you feel devalued personally, but you
feel devalued in the sense of your religion. Did I just go against
God? Am I eternally screwed?"

This young woman went on to flip-flop in her opinion
about whether to have sex or not, whether she wanted to have
sex or not, and whether God's approval was more important
to her than what she wanted to do on a personal level. "It's
biblically stated that you are to remain a virgin until marriage,"
she said. "But then I look at that almost in a historical context,
because the Bible was written so long ago, and times have
changed so much that it's almost as if it doesn't really matter,
does it?"

Although God isn't much of a factor in the average college
student's decisions about sex, their peers are a factor—indeed,

a major factor. Peer opinion is enough to sway them about the types of sexual intimacy they should engage in and what they can legitimately hold back. Virginity is not something determined by one's religion, God, or a wider community of adults, parents, teachers, or ministers. Instead, it is determined by personal experience, trial and error, and the need to either participate or have something to hold back within hookup culture.

Most students defined virginity in traditional heterosexual terms, but there were several students who offered three separate categories of what it means to "lose" one's virginity based on sexual orientation: oral sex if a person identifies as a lesbian, anal sex if a person identifies as gay, and heterosexual intercourse if a person identifies as straight.

"I think [you can do] everything up until intercourse," said one student, referring to both heterosexual and gay intercourse in relation to virginity. "I'm not really sure where the line is drawn for girls, though, because they have *two* means of intercourse. I know it's perceived for girls that if it's anal, then it's not really their virginity, but then, it's still intercourse, so I don't know how I feel about that." Then there was the issue of whether oral sex counted as sex or not for this young man, a student at a secular university. As with so many of his peers, it was a complicated topic for him, because he also considered oral sex as a compromise that could allow students to say they legitimately participated in hookup culture while still claiming virginity. "[Oral sex] is a way to be like, 'We had a certain form of sex, but it wasn't intercourse,'" he explained. "There's the whole base system, and [oral sex] is before the sex, the intercourse stage. So I feel like it's something that happens if you're not really at the intercourse stage. Maybe you would feel more comfortable [engaging in oral sex] if you had a guilty conscious about having sex with someone." Then he added: "I think maybe in the gay community it's more prominent for oral sex to happen before *real* sex."

ONE YOUNG MAN I SPOKE WITH, named Gabriel, who was gay, had used his status as a virgin to opt out of hookup culture until he felt he was ready for sex.[4] He had wanted to wait for sex until he was in love, and he was proud to speak about this goal. Eventually, he had happily achieved it. Being a virgin, in his opinion, had given him the right to wait for love; once a person had sex, he said, that right was lost. Gabriel joked several times that when he was a virgin he had felt as though a choir burst into song each time he had walked into a room, announcing his innocence to everyone within earshot. "It depends on who you're with, but it can be anything from like, 'Oh my gosh, you're such a saint!' to, 'That's really too bad you haven't had sex yet.'"

Gabriel's peers had assumed that people who were still virgins during college had "to be pious." "In most cases," he said, there was "a religious reason behind [virginity]." Gabriel had quickly become accustomed to this sort of reaction, but he had not been afraid to talk about his status as a virgin gay man on campus. He said, "I do a panel for this group on campus, and we play a game called Guess the Straight Person. One of the people on the panel isn't gay, and people in the audience have to ask questions to see if they can figure out who is straight. A lot of the questions end up turning sexual, like, 'What's your favorite position?' And I'd be like, 'Oh, I haven't had sex yet,' and people in the audience would be like, '*Awwwwww!*'"

Gabriel was aware that his status as a virgin had been unusual, but he also displayed an unusually high level of confidence about his sexual identity. He believed his peers were the unenlightened ones, and that he really knew how to make sex work during the college experience. If anything, he had felt more amused by his peers' reactions to his status as virgin than anything, even superior to them because of it, and he was quick to disavow their pity. "It's not a sad thing, and it's not because I'm not attractive enough or because I couldn't if I wanted to," he said. He'd always planned on waiting for the right guy, and he got to live out this fantasy, making him one of the few students I interviewed who reminisced about first-time sex as if it was one of the most blissful moments of his life so far.

"I've dated a lot of people and I had a boyfriend freshman year and we were both in a committed monogamous relationship," Gabriel said, recalling past experiences that didn't lead to sex:

> He really wanted to have sex, and for some reason I just *knew* it wasn't right. I wanted to have sex in general, and I was totally enamored of him, but I knew that something was wrong,

too. Maybe it was just that I knew it wasn't going to work out, that we weren't going to stay together. I ended up breaking up with him at the end of the semester. I would have been devastated had I lost my virginity to him, knowing that he couldn't give me what I needed. So I think it's really important for me to be able to say that I used my judgment, that I didn't give that piece of myself to him because he didn't deserve it.

Although Gabriel had been close to having sex his freshman year, he still had a long wait before he'd meet that perfect guy. "Sophomore year I did not kiss a soul, and then junior year, when I was abroad, I made out with two boys," he said. "Then when I came back I met my current boyfriend, and he's just someone that I wanted to be serious with, and I began to think, 'I'm mature enough, I think I'm there!' A lot of it for me is being ready." For Gabriel, being "ready" involved many considerations, most of which extended beyond the physical desire to have sex. They included the approval of the relationship from both families as well as the promise of a future together. Best of all, for Gabriel, was that his boyfriend turned out to be a virgin, too. This thrilled him, even though his friends had warned him not to have sex for the first time with another virgin, the preconception being that if two virgins had sex, it would inevitably be bad sex.

"[My boyfriend and I] talked about it beforehand. It wasn't like one night we were making out and we had sex. We dated for about four or five months before it happened," he said about their first time. "The only way I was willing to lose my virginity was by knowing that it was going to be a spiritual connection and knowing that it was going to bring that person and I closer and not push us apart."

Gabriel was one of the most empowered, emotionally secure students I interviewed during the study. His pride in his first sexual experience said something else important: that good, romantic, loving, committed, fulfilling sex was a rarity during college and within hookup culture. In Gabriel's opinion, most people "settle" and have sex that is "just okay," or even altogether "meaningless" and random. His status as a virgin ultimately worked in his favor—it kept him out of hookup culture long enough that he was able to find sexual fulfillment in a more meaningful way for him.

There is a sex-positive interpretation of Gabriel's language about "giving away a piece of himself" as characteristic of what it meant to lose his virginity: because Gabriel viewed his virginity as something precious, he used this status to hold out for great first-time sex. To have sex as a virgin or with a virgin is to accept the possibility of engaging in meaningful sex. Many teens and young adults understand virginity in similar, sex-positive ways and use virginity as a negotiating tool to help decide the when, the where, the how, and the who of first-time sex. Even in the midst of hookup culture, some students consider virginity as sacred and first-time sex as a worthy possession. For these students, this worthy possession can become their right to expect good, fulfilling, even loving, committed sex on the emotional, physical, and spiritual levels. They suspect that sex can be pleasurable, meaningful, exciting, emotionally vulnerable, and connective—at the very least, that sex can be better than the kind offered by a hookup—and so they wait.

Everyone knows that first-time sex is a big deal, and many young adults understand losing their virginity as a make-or-break situation. Although this notion worked in Gabriel's favor, the view of virginity as a "precious object" that will be gone after first-time sex does not always lead to a happy ending, however. It makes the decision for first-time sex a very high-stakes matter and a possible source of tremendous regret and shame. There is only one first person with whom you have sex, one first time for sex, which means you have only one chance to get this right or wrong. Most adolescents agonize over the when, the where, the how, and the who before they make the decision to engage in sex for the first time. Many also have a lengthy checklist in mind that must be fulfilled before they embark on this experience. This checklist may include such considerations as how old they will be, the setting (after the prom, before graduation, on the beach, on a particularly starry night), how long they will have been with their partner, or whether there is mutual love between them.

The average student's talk of virginity as a "thing" to offer someone else, as if virginity were literally a mark on the body, or something in the body that a person can give away or take, can become problematic: it is exactly the kind of culturally constructed, gendered talk that leads teens and young adults to think that once they "give themselves away" there is no going back. According to this language, virginity is a fragile, special thing that you "possess," and if there is any misstep with it, you could be ruined forever. When words like "gift" and "piece" and "loss" arise, they indicate how high the stakes are for this one sexual encounter in a person's life. Especially in traditional religious contexts, but also within hookup culture, the "price" or "cost" of virginity is often perceived as affecting one's entire future.[5]

Once their virginity is "gone"—once they've made this all-important decision and had this once-in-a-lifetime experience—many young adults typically can't find a good enough reason to stop being sexually active—even if the sex wasn't good, or they didn't feel good about it. Between culture and religion, we've layered so much importance onto first-time sex that for many students, *any* sex that follows afterward seems irrelevant and not worth caring about. Virginity can offer a helpful boundary for some students, whereas for others, virginity loss has a negative effect on future sexual decision-making. Few students that I interviewed could speak about good sex from personal experience, yet many continued having sex anyway, often for the purpose of simply being able to say to their peers that they were having it.

In her 2009 book *The Purity Myth: How America's Obsession with Virginity Is Hurting Young Women*, Jessica Valenti offered a lengthy, eloquent argument that virginity does not exist at all and is instead a cultural construction that creates countless problems, injustices, and oppressive circumstances for young women today.[6] Valenti suggested that we do away with the concept of virginity altogether. Her argument is powerful, and I found it especially so as I listened to college students use such high-stakes language to describe their sexual status. The double standard about men, women, and sex is laden throughout their virginity talk, as are the sometimes disturbing implications for self-esteem and communal perception.

Yet, despite Valenti's critique, there are still too many students who *need* virginity—who use it toward the end of sexual empowerment, turning it into a helpful boundary—to dismiss it out of hand as Valenti did. And while some students see virginity loss as a reason to continue having sex even if they feel bad about it, there are others who react in the opposite way: young adults who have already become sexually active but who come back to virginity for a second time as a helpful model for putting the brakes on their sex life in the future.

One young man I interviewed who was no longer a virgin did just this—he had entered into a temporary second virginity, of sorts. This student, Jamie, who was a senior, had taken a step back from having sex.[7] He had decided to hold out for good, meaningful sex, and his experience had told him that hookups were not the means to this end. His perception was that everyone on his Catholic college campus hooked up— he'd done it as well—yet by his last year in college he had found himself among friends who were more like him who valued relationships.

A short time before we met for our interview, Jamie had been in a long-term relationship. When he and his girlfriend of two years broke up (his "first love," he called her), the loss had sent him into a tailspin and straight into hookup culture. "I found myself in a really rough place mentally and emotionally," he wrote in his journal. "Drinking was taken to a new level, and I did not take much stake in anything that was happening. I was in a place where I would have done most anything. This reckless abandon is not something I find enjoyable. . . . Physical happenings devoid of emotional connection are just nowhere near as fruitful as an intimate, emotional exchange between people."

During our conversation about this time in his life, Jamie described himself as a "loose cannon" and said that he had not been engaged in "any moral decision making at that point." Jamie wrote about how one of the most disappointing things about someone you've been with sexually was to find out afterward that she wasn't interested in you emotionally. He felt that he shouldn't regret these experiences, because he didn't "feel that looking back and trying to change something [was] a worthwhile pursuit," but he also wrote about his regrets during those months.

"To a lot of people, [sex] can be a very light thing, in terms of its meaning," he wrote. "I would say in general, the crew of people I hang out with on an everyday basis don't take it as something light and that just happens. On a personal level, I think it is something that can be very meaningful." With Jamie's former girlfriend, sex had not only been great and fulfilling, he said during out interview, but he felt that with her he had learned what "making love" meant.[8] To have a wonderful sex life for so long and then have only hookup sex was a rude awakening.

Sex was a complicated issue for just about everyone, according to Jamie, whether you were a virgin, a non-virgin, or someone who'd had great sex with one person and then suddenly had to move on, as he had. "I give a lot of credit to people who are able to be aware of themselves enough to only engage in sexual activity when they feel it is completely right," he wrote. He was referring especially to friends of his who had always been able to refrain from hooking up even when they were feeling low, lonely, unattractive, and lost. Jamie wished he lived on a campus where men could be more open about their feelings—"less antisentimental," as he put it—and who took sex more seriously overall. "I don't think that a lot of men are comfortable saying they are a virgin. A lot of guys see it as unacceptable." In Jamie's opinion, most men were taught to be uncomfortable about love and were permitted to talk about it only on a superficial level, at best.

Between Jamie's breakup and the time he wrote his journal for the study, his period of being a "loose cannon" had ended. He had made a new resolution about his sex life—that it would be tied exclusively to being in love from there on out. He wrote about how he now spent entire afternoons daydreaming about relationships and that he had become hopeful again about his future romantic prospects. Plus, he thought he had a pretty good handle on the woman he was looking for. Jamie reasserted that he wanted to find someone he could "continually fall in love with" day after day, conversation after conversation, as he had with his former girlfriend. For him, love was fundamentally about human connection, truly getting to know someone else and being known, and he felt that this should extend to how you expressed romantic feeling. He wasn't interested in romancing just any girl, either, but *the* girl, and he was determined to wait for her and for love for as long as it took. In other words, he'd pressed "pause" on his sex life.

Jamie was no longer a virgin, yet he had stepped into a sphere of temporary virginity by deciding that he only wanted to have sex again if he was in love with and committed to his partner, a decision he discussed at length during our interview. He had thereby effectively and consciously opted out of the culture around him. What is interesting about those students who hang onto virginity, or someone like Jamie, who hangs onto the hope of meaningful sex, is that all of them have been sexually active to some degree—and want to continue to be sexually active to some degree as well. Hanging onto one's status as a virgin, at least "technically," is one of the most common methods of participating in hookup culture while simultaneously opting out of at least part of it. Students feel they can be sexually active to a point, yet their virginity gives them the right to step away when a hookup reaches a certain level of sexual intimacy. Virginity, in these instances, offers them an excuse to hold back from fully entering the world of the hookup. It functions as one of the only boundaries left within hookup culture—a boundary that at least some students use to negotiate their sexual decision-making.

Virginity—whether temporary or reclaimed—is a boundary that many students use to negotiate their own love story of sorts, to hang onto the possibility of love in their future, and this despite hookup culture. Virginity is a tool they use to live in hookup culture, and even be an active participant in it, gaining themselves that social cache they so long for, while still making decisions about the extent of sexual intimacy they will engage in. Virginity is a bargaining chip on both individual and communal levels—it is a person's right to hang onto it if they so choose, and a method of hanging onto a little bit of sexual power. And whatever helps students expand their sense of rights around sex in the middle of hookup culture is valuable indeed.

Chapter Seven

Opting Out:
Rethinking Abstinence in
the Age of Hookup Culture

*Those who do not adhere to—and particularly
those who publicly question—the tenets or practices
of [hookup] culture are thus considered unaccepted,
unwelcome, and abnormal.*

—THE ANSCOMBE SOCIETY, PRINCETON UNIVERSITY

A FEW YEARS AGO, I was invited to participate in a roundtable for *Christianity Today*. Three contributors were asked, "What's the best way to encourage people to save sex for the covenant of marriage?"[1] I agreed to write a piece for the roundtable, with the caveat that I couldn't honestly answer a question about how to convince people to "save sex for the covenant of marriage" without explaining that I didn't like the question. My fellow respondents were Mark Regnerus, author of *Forbidden Fruit: Sex and Religion in the Lives of American Teenagers*, which provides an overview of data on sex, faith, and teenagers that grew out of Christian Smith's National Study of Youth and Religion (NSYR), and Richard Ross, the cofounder of True Love Waits, the most famous and viral of the abstinence pledge programs popular among evangelical youth.[2]

Regnerus began his answer by noting that "the time gap between sexual maturity and marriage is the highest it's ever been." The evangelical response, he said, had been inadequate: "Evangelicals muster popular perspectives on courtship and what clothes can and cannot come off and when. The lack of an authoritative message about sexuality is not lost on youth." His comments could be read as an implicit critique of programs like True Love Waits. Regnerus's tack was to offer a reminder that "saving sex for marriage" is a process based on "an intended order" of activities: "a pledge of fidelity, reliability, integrity, and friendship between a man and a woman, a covenant between the two persons and God, a communal recognition of the marriage." All of this comes first, and *then* there is "sexual consummation," and the consummation is always heterosexual. According to Regnerus, "There's no such thing as premarital sex. There is only non-marital sex and marital sex. When couples skip some of the steps, it's the job of the church to make sure the others occur, or to call non-marital sex the sacrilege it is."[3]

Richard Ross appealed to piety and mounted a defense of his purity pledge program. True Love Waits works, he said, despite recent studies that show otherwise.[4] "True Love Waits is not a promise to a program, card, or ring," he wrote:

It is a sincere promise of purity made to the reigning Christ for the glory of the Father by the power of the Spirit.

The promise is kept most tenaciously by teenagers who have moved beyond moralistic therapeutic deism and who adore the King of Kings with awe and intimacy. They know their Lord and Savior said, "If you love me, you will keep my commandments." Their walk in purity is a way to express deep love for him and to respond to his supremacy.

For teenagers who know Christ, that is a far stronger motivator than a desire to avoid disease and pregnancy.

For Ross, Jesus holds all the cards. Ross accordingly argued that "the most powerful way to impact prom-night decisions is for parents, leaders, and peers to more fully awaken teenagers to God's Son, to invite them to make a promise to him, and to walk beside them in a journey toward purity."

Regnerus offered a "back to the basics" approach, or even a "stick to the basics" one. It involves encouraging young Christians to discern what their "calling" is—"marriage or singleness"—and then supporting their efforts to follow that calling. Ross advocated for his program, True Love Waits: tell teenagers that Jesus wants them to "walk in purity," and, if they stick with Jesus, then they will be able to walk this walk, plain and simple.

For many evangelical young adults, both Regnerus's and Ross's responses have real traction. Ross's might have the most of all, since the True Love Waits program, which packages purity with all the bells and whistles that Regnerus despises, is appealing to a large segment of the Christian youth population, at least while they are still very young.[5] But promoting abstinence from a religiously conservative standpoint—preaching no sexual intimacy until marriage—has traction only among teens for whom faith is the central, decision-making frame for all aspects of their life.

These arguments and their corresponding methods fall on deaf ears among the average teen and college student population—students who are not evangelical, who do not live in tight faith communities of peers all hoping to "save sex for marriage," and who do not accept conservative views about sex from the political right. In fact, the people of many faiths hold strict views of sex and chastity—including not only evangelicals but also Muslims, Mormons, and Orthodox Jews. For those outside of these communities, most, if not all, of this chastity talk is seen as irrelevant. Simply offering all young adults a future of "saving sex for marriage" is not an effective response to hookup culture. It is extreme to the point that students cannot imagine living it, nor do they wish to. In addition, it leaves gay, lesbian, and bisexual students completely out of the picture. Most young adults want to be sexually active by the time they get to college, and most want to retain some agency and control over their sexual decision-making. This makes *Christianity Today*'s question about how to convince youth to "save sex for marriage" largely a pointless, misguided task in such contexts.

Yet there is a growing, vocal minority of sexually conservative college students at some of the nation's most prestigious universities who are standing up for exactly this—saving sex for marriage. These students are not at evangelical institutions, where chastity is the norm and hookup culture doesn't exist, but have chosen to attend the Catholic, private-secular, and public institutions that are currently immersed in hookup culture. These students are determined to live sexually conservative values despite hookup culture's dominance, and they want to provide like-minded students on their campuses with a visible, viable means for opting out. My first lecture visit to Princeton University was on the invitation of one of these student groups, the Anscombe Society, which has made substantial media headlines about its conservative sexual ethos. Since the society was formed in 2005, the commitment of its members to chastity until marriage and traditional values has both fascinated and horrified their Princeton peers, faculty members, and the university administration. It has also captured the imagination of a wider public.

According to the society's mission statement, the Anscombe Society "is a student organization at Princeton University dedicated to affirming the importance of the family, marriage, and a proper understanding for the role of sex and sexuality." The document echoes both Regnerus and Ross, though without any explicitly religious language: "We aim to promote an environment that values . . . a chaste lifestyle which respects and appreciates human sexuality, relationships, and dignity.

Therefore, we celebrate sex as unifying, beautiful, and joyful when shared in its proper context: that of marriage between a man and woman."[6] A separate document includes a short description of the reasoning behind the foundation of Anscombe: "In the face of the hook-up culture, the Anscombe Society has been dedicated to providing support for abstinent students at Princeton since the society's inception in 2005."

It didn't take long for Anscombe's membership to grow, and the society became a loud presence on campus, despite its insistence that the only "proper context" for sex is marriage, and despite declaring that marriage is "between a man and a woman," when Princeton has a proudly "out" gay and lesbian population. The media found it freakishly interesting that such a group would not only exist at an Ivy League school but succeed in becoming more and more popular. College students loudly proclaiming their commitment to abstinence until marriage in a very "abstinence-only education" way seemed strange in the context of a popular culture that expects college campuses to sustain an ethic of casual sex.

Skepticism about the society has permeated articles about it in the mainstream media. One of the first pieces appeared in the *New York Times* in April 2005 with the headline, "A Group at Princeton Where 'No' Means 'Entirely No,'" as though the very idea that students existed who did not want to be hooking up was surprising. "Members of the Anscombe Society maintain that campus life has become so drenched in sexuality, from the flavored condoms handed out by a resident adviser to the social pressure of the hookup scene, that Princeton needs a voice arguing for traditional sexual values," wrote Iver Peterson about why Anscombe formed on campus. "For the Princeton students, the idea is simply to be heard in an atmosphere that not only condones sexual activity among young adults, but, they maintain, expects it."[7] Other headlines, such as "Abstinence Comes to the Ivy League?" from MSNBC.com, "Princeton Virgins Don't Take Sex-Education Club Lying Down" in the *Boston Herald*, and "Girls Gone Mild" in the *Philadelphia Daily News*, led with surprise that the concept of chastity even still existed.[8]

Once Anscombe got off the ground, it wasn't long before groups with like-minded politics and sexual ethos began to emerge at other premier institutions of higher education, most famously at Harvard with True Love Revolution in 2006, which provoked a similar media frenzy both on campus and beyond. The Massachusetts Institute of Technology followed suit with its own Anscombe Society, which encouraged students to think hard about sex and its purpose and place in their lives, and which promoted chastity as the only true path toward a healthy attitude about sex.[9] More satellite Anscombe Societies were established, especially after Cassandra Hough, a founding member of Anscombe at Princeton, started an organization called the Love & Fidelity Network in 2007. The Network is also based in Princeton, New Jersey, and its website advertises its concern that the "discussion inside and outside of the classroom has become increasingly one-sided on questions of sex, love, and relationships." Love & Fidelity's mission is to "to educate, train, and equip college students with the arguments, resources, and direction they need to uphold the institution of marriage, the unique role of the family, and sexual integrity on their campuses."[10]

The Network regularly brings together students from campuses all over the country to discuss their like-minded political values and provide support and guidance for fledging Anscombe Societies—and these societies are cropping up at institutions everywhere. The Providence College chapter, for example, founded in January 2010, "hopes to truly engage in a counter-culture movement that will bring back the true meaning of love, fidelity, and the upholding of the true dignity of each person."[11] All of these campus societies are a direct response to hookup culture and try to offer a publicly identified space for heterosexual students who want to opt out of it.

With the help of the Love & Fidelity Network, Princeton's Anscombe Society went so far as to propose an on-campus Abstinence Center that would provide services, conversation, and activities for students interested in an alternative to hookup culture. "The dominant sexual ethos at Princeton University is the 'hook-up culture,' a lifestyle of casual sex and uncommitted relationships," wrote society members in their proposal. "Under this culture, the lifestyle of hooking up is presented not merely as normal, but also as normative. Those who do not adhere to—and particularly those who publicly question—

the tenets or practices of this culture are thus considered unaccepted, unwelcome, and abnormal. . . . As a result, students
at Princeton who wish to remain abstinent not only face im-
mense social pressure to conform to the hook-up culture, but
many also find themselves stigmatized, marginalized, and alienated when they do not." Anscombe sought a place on campus
that "would provide chaste students with concrete [institutional]
support" within the "troubled waters of college sexual culture."
Abstinent students at Princeton experience "localized discrimination," as the society members put it. The center would work
to correct "the cultural perception that students with chaste
ethical views are somehow abnormal."[12]

GIVEN WIDESPREAD COMPLAINTS by students about being
stuck in hookup culture, the rise of organizations like Anscombe
and the Love & Fidelity Network makes sense. There is an audience for them, not only among conservative and religious
students, but also among students who are uncomfortable with
hookup culture for a variety of personal reasons. Pervasive silence and passivity in the face of hookup culture could not last
forever. That the dissenting voice emerged from the political
right isn't remarkable either. It was logical for vocal anti-
hookup-culture groups like Anscombe to declare themselves
socially, politically, and religiously conservative. These societies'
members see themselves as providing an alternative view of sex
in the face of the liberal politics they believe to be at the bottom
of hookup culture—that is, the feminist movement, the sexual

revolution, and liberal-leaning, antireligious values. They have placed themselves at the opposite end of the political spectrum.

These societies also come with a right-wing veneer of heterosexist, antigay leanings. This is unfortunate, because it serves to alienate the larger, silent majority of students on most university campuses who are not happy with hookup culture but would never align themselves with such politics. The politically moderate to liberal student either would not or simply could not consider the Anscombe version of abstinence, either, because it does not fit their politics in general. They also may not want to wait until marriage to have sex, even though they do not like the extreme hookup culture in which they find themselves.

There is a vocal, public opposition to Anscombe and the Love & Fidelity Network among other Princeton students. A columnist in the university's student newspaper, *The Daily Princetonian,* argued that the society was misguided because it promoted antigay bigotry.[13] Anscombe's proposal for the Abstinence Center was defeated, in part, for this very reason. The members of the society complained about discrimination against chaste students, but embedded in their proposal were discriminatory attitudes about same-sex relationships.

Princeton University's president, Shirley Tilghman, rejected Anscombe's Abstinence Center proposal primarily for its heterosexism. But she also decided that the Anscombe students' claim about feeling stigmatized, and even discriminated against, was overblown. This was an unfortunate, unsympathetic response on her part, in my opinion.[14] Such dismissals only support the continued dominance of hookup culture. Students who are suffering in the midst of hookup culture suffer ridicule already, and such judgments only make their plight worse. Just because a faculty member or college administrator does not like a student group's politics does not mean that these same students should be left to struggle on their own.

A better response from Princeton would have been to challenge Anscombe to broaden its scope and definition of abstinence beyond right-wing religious politics and to explicitly include same-sex relationships. The Princeton administration failed the broader Princeton student body by not helping Anscombe to expand its conversation to be more inclusive. Politics aside, the Anscombe students are not alone in feeling lost amid hookup culture. The Princeton administration certainly failed this group by not empowering them to discuss why and how they experienced isolation on their campus.

Because the conversation around Anscombe and similar societies gets caught up in politics, it misses their significance as a response to hookup culture. These groups represent the only organized, visible effort to directly and explicitly address student unease about hookup culture on college campuses thus far. It is student-generated responses that have the greatest potential to help ease the strains that young people feel within hookup culture. Every college and university I have visited has been searching for practical and visible structures for offering students alternatives to hookup culture and support when they are distressed or disappointed by it. With some serious rethinking and broad political input, Anscombe's Center for Abstinence could have become a model response. The same goes for the Anscombe Societies cropping up nationwide: these groups want to provide an alternative space and social life for students who do not want their lives dominated by hookup culture. Such groups are needed, and although their missions court only the conservative population on campus, the college community should recognize that they are a start.

Like so many others, the left-leaning feminist in me recoils at the way these groups rail against the women's movement and homosexuality, too. But the scholar in me, having spent years listening to the concerns of teens and young adults, knows not to allow student politics to overshadow the fact that they also have something valuable to tell us. The young people who form these societies live within hookup culture just like everyone else and deserve an attentive ear. They feel coerced, silenced, and stuck in the norms of hookup culture. They have every right to voice these feelings and to receive respectful attention. Students may turn a deaf ear when someone talks at them with a teaching they do not like, but faculty, staff, and college administrators have a responsibility to care for and try to help all students, politics aside.

THE REACTION TO PRO-ABSTINENCE student groups on campus has coincided with attitudes about abstinence in general in the larger society, especially in the context of the sex-education culture wars. Given the movement to install abstinence-only education programs in America's public schools during President George W. Bush's term in office, and more recently the controversies raging over President Barack Obama's health-care legislation, this debate is primarily divided along party lines.

Republicans claim that teaching teenagers about condoms will encourage them to have sex, that birth-control pills cause abortions, and that federal funding should never go toward anything related to abortion. Abstinence discussed within a conservative faith context is always linked to marriage and is often interpreted to extremes, as in Richard Ross's True Love Waits program. Abstinence, within Christian purity culture, may not only mean refraining from oral, anal, and vaginal intercourse, but extend to kissing, holding hands, and even having lustful thoughts about a person who is not your spouse (or future spouse).[15] Religious conservatives have successfully woven strains of such interpretations into sex-education programs in schools across the United States. As a result, politically moderate and liberal-leaning people have turned a deaf ear on the word "abstinence" itself. The politics around abstinence-only education has turned people off to the possibility that there could be any fruitful, alternative conversation around abstinence aside from the conservative right-wing one.[16]

But rather than wage war over whether abstinence education works, it may be more important to wonder what is behind the investment of so many scholars and the media in defeating abstinence education. Rather than reclaiming abstinence, or re-envisioning it for more moderate views, we have simply thrown it out altogether. In the process, we have allowed a single, politically interested, religious group to own the word. Our society suffers from a lack of serious reflection on what practicing abstinence might look like, and how the many ways of living abstinence might benefit a broad segment of the young adult population.

When we choose to focus on politics instead of the lived experiences of teens and college students, we are ignoring the complex realities of a generation. These young adults are attempting to navigate life within hookup culture—they are working hard to negotiate this new realm of sexuality—and they are ending up feeling lost because we are not giving them the support they need. Amid the culture wars over sex and abstinence-only education, we are neglecting questions about whether sex can be meaningful at all after first-time sex. We are also overlooking the many types of meaningful sex that are possible. We offer young adults a million reasons to think before they do it the first time, and a million reasons to worry about the negative repercussions of sex (STIs, pregnancy, God, etc.), but we do not give them reasons to value sex in general.

While the left focuses on promoting safe sex and making sure teens understand its mechanics, and the right is busy trying to convince teens to erase any trace of sexual desire until marriage, a shocking gap in the conversation about sex has opened up. This gap has grown so wide that when young adults arrive at college, they fall right through it and keep on falling. These students do not have much of an idea what sex means to them personally. It's difficult not to wonder what would happen if the right no longer owned abstinence. Why haven't we rethought, expanded, and even redefined abstinence to serve a far wider population of teens and young adults, those who *are* interested in being sexually active, regardless of their marital status or sexual orientation, yet who get pulled into hookup culture and don't know how to get themselves out?

To go back to the roundtable hosted by *Christianity Today* with Mark Regnerus, Richard Ross, and myself, my response was to rephrase the question with a nonevangelical, nondevout young adult audience in mind: "Given hookup culture, what's the best way to foster an alternative conversation about abstinence?"

Reasoning about abstinence does not have to serve an agenda that involves convincing people that there is a "proper container" (like marriage) for sex, which turns out to be a "container" that excludes gay and lesbian couples in most states. In conversations about abstinence, the priority should be the health and well-being of teens and young adults. Many teens and young adults make their decisions about sex, whether to have it, and how far to go as if marriage had nothing to do with sex.[17] How can we foster new ideas for practicing abstinence that fit this shift in attitudes? It is a question worth our consideration, because so many young adults are looking for a way out of hookup culture.

Lately I have begun to talk a lot about abstinence when I am on various campuses for lecture visits. The most important thing I try to convey to students is the following: just because you've had sex once or many times (however you define sex) does not mean you need to *keep* having it; no longer being a virgin (however you define virginity) does not mean that you may as well keep hooking up, because after your first time, all sex becomes meaningless; if the sex you are having is not as good as you hoped it might be, it's all right to stop and give yourself time to think about what good sex is and how you might go after it; there is not a single reason to continue having sex and/or to continue to hook up if it is not fulfilling.[18]

Even committed student couples assume that once they've started having sex, they need to keep having it, even if it isn't very good—especially if their relationship grew out of a serial hookup. Giving a couple a reason to pause—the right to take time out from the sex they are already having, to spend time discussing and reflecting on the sex they'd like to be having—could make all the difference. Abstinence, understood as pressing "pause" on one's sex life, can be an empowering thing to do for to oneself, for one's sex life, and even for one's current or future partner(s).

Practicing temporary abstinence is its own form of sexual experimentation. We usually think of sexual experimentation as trying out different positions, à la the *Kama Sutra*, but this is an impoverished way of envisioning the idea. There is no reason why sexual experimentation should exclude periods of abstinence, and our ideas about it need to be broad enough to include trying on abstinence. This trial can be for as little as a single weekend, for the very purpose of thinking about how to have good sex in the near future. Choosing not to hook up for a short period of time does not require a sudden, heroic commitment to abstinence until a person finds his or her life partner. Sometimes all it takes is for a young adult to be given a reasonable option—taking one weekend off—and suddenly, a realistic option for trying abstinence is on the table, as well as a viable excuse to opt out of hookup culture for a bit.

Advocating periods of temporary abstinence to teens and young adults who are interested in continuing to be sexually active could make all the difference in their ability to find the fulfillment they seek from sex, to find a way through and even out from under hookup culture's dominance, and to think about their sexual identity and practices.

To pursue this path, we must be willing not only to enter into the conversation that already exists on abstinence, but also to expand it to include all teens and young adults, regardless of sexual orientation. This conversation should include those who will want to continue to have sex, irrespective of marriage, but who may simply want to rethink the sex they are currently having. Abstinence does not *have* to be inextricably linked to marriage. That we have allowed it to be limited in this way is a failure of liberal and moderate thinkers, politicians, and academics to think imaginatively, for fear of becoming associ-ated with the religious right. This stubborn refusal to engage—except to dig in one's heels on the opposite end of the political spectrum—comes at an unacceptable cost, especially given the potential benefits to our students of the dialogue we could be having.

Choosing abstinence, if only temporarily, could become one of the most subversive, profoundly effective tools teens and young adults had. It is abstinence within reason. It is ab-stinence that makes sense, given the sexual activity that young adults already engage in. It is abstinence that college students can actually practice. And it is abstinence that might, just might, lead to good sex whenever an individual has decided that he or she is ready for it.

Chapter Eight

Opting Out of Hookup Culture
via The Date

I'm a guy and I've never asked out a girl.
—SENIOR MAN AT A PRIVATE-SECULAR UNIVERSITY

Hooking up is like a trial run. It's like,
we're gonna skip all that first date stuff and
see if that was worth having the first date.
—SENIOR MAN AT A PRIVATE-SECULAR UNIVERSITY

I feel like it's hard to take the first meeting
of a girl anywhere.
—JUNIOR MAN AT A PRIVATE-SECULAR UNIVERSITY

"DATING IS ALMOST UNHEARD OF to me at this point," said one junior woman from a secular university. "Sometimes you'll be hooking up with three different guys or you'll be hooking up with all three at once. I don't really hear about people going to a dinner and a movie."

157

"I've never gone on a date here," said another young woman, a senior, also from a secular school. "I don't feel like people date anymore. I don't hear, 'Oh I went on a date with so-and-so last night.' It's not as formal as it used to be. I feel like my generation has a general idea of what dating should be from TV. The guy asked you out and you go out to dinner, a movie. I don't feel like that happens so much at college. You either meet up at a party or you hang out at their house." She wasn't very satisfied with this situation. "I think girls want to be taken out on dates, I really do," she went on. "My friends and I have talked about this before. I really want go on a date to see what it's like. . . . We don't think it's any different than just hanging out, but you get dressed up to go out on a date. It seems like such an odd idea, because we don't, *I* don't do that. My friends don't do that."

A young woman at a Catholic college had similar comments about the apparent absence of dating on her campus. "I actually haven't seen any people go dating, a guy and a girl going out by themselves. That seems like more after you have decided you are together," she said, referring to the fact that if people did ever date, it was only after they had started a long-term relationship, usually after months of engaging in a serial hookup.

A woman at one of the secular universities echoed this idea: "If people are dating, it's more like they're just hooking up with the same person for an extended period of time, rather than they are in a relationship with them. Most people are single." When I asked her why most people were single at her school, she had a difficult time answering the question. "I don't know. I have been single for a while now and I still can't figure it out. If I could *not* be single, I would not be single, because then I wouldn't have to worry about dating for a while. I think people like to make it hard on themselves. I can't figure it out. If I could, then I wouldn't be single right now."

Other students echoed her feelings, too. Generally, students felt that they were not in control of the decision to date or not to date, or to be single or in a relationship. They felt that hookup culture dictated for them that there would be no dating, and that they simply had to endure this reality. They concluded that they had to let go of any desire they may have harbored to date their way into a relationship in a more traditional manner.

A first-year student at a Catholic college spoke at length about the absence of dating on her campus. Like the student quoted above, she felt she didn't know how to begin a real relationship. Part of the problem was the fear of rejection. In her view, people covered up for this lack of knowledge (about how to get into a relationship) and its accompanying anxieties by drinking. "People feel that when they are drunk they don't have to worry about what they are doing . . . that they don't have as big a chance of rejection," she said. Alcohol helped to dull their embarrassment and their fear that the other party might not be interested in them and allowed them to hide their nervousness about being around people for whom they had real feelings.

The idea that "nobody ever dates here" was one of the most common refrains of my study, and it is something I continue to hear constantly from students on campus lecture visits. When I conducted the formal, face-to-face interviews, the students, one after the other, would bemoan the lack of a dating culture on campus. At the same time, they complained that they were probably the only one who mourned this absence. I found myself wanting to tell each student before they exited the room: "By the way, when you go through that door, someone is going to be waiting to come in and see me. Take good notice of them. If you think they're cute, ask them out. Chances are they wish to go out on dates just like you do. If they're not your type, keep coming back to check people out. I'm here all week!"

Occasionally, during the Q&A after one of my lectures, a college administrator will stand up and ask students if indeed this is true, and a lot of nodding heads inevitably follow. That hookups are the only option is implicit in this perception about why there is an absence of dating on campus. It becomes a self-fulfilling prophecy. Nobody dates because they think nobody else wants to date, and these cycles go round and round again. And this feeds the perpetuation of hookup culture.

Out of 68 students from Catholic, private-secular, and public schools who commented at length about the dating scene on their campus during formal interviews, 37 (54 percent) of these students claimed that dating was uncommon or even unheard of on their campuses. An additional 23 (34 percent) said that they thought the scene was mixed at their school: there were a lot of people involved in long-term relationships, especially the older students on campus (juniors and seniors), but a large part of the campus population was highly invested in hooking up as well. Then there were 8 students (12 percent) who said they felt that dating was common at their colleges—but when most of these students spoke about what this dating was like, it turned out that they did not mean that people went out on traditional dates, but that they had managed to make their way into long-term, committed relationships via a serial hookup. Of the 68 students who spoke about dating, 16 of them (24 percent) went on to comment that they believed women on campus cared more about going out on dates than men do, and only 2 students (less than 1 percent) said they felt that both men and women cared the same amount about dating.

One young man, a junior at a secular university, explained his theory about why women wanted to be in relationships more than men did, but ended up hooking up anyway. "I think it gets ingrained in their mind that there's no chance that I'm going to find anyone to date. I might as well just give in and do what the guy wants and what the guy wants is, you know, to hook up. I think people lower their expectations and their standards when they are in college." A first-year woman at a Catholic college felt that women, in particular, lost out when it came to finding dates. "For a guy, there are girls everywhere, so why would they settle with one girl?" she said. "A lot of girls get tied into open relationships where they will basically be with one guy, but the guy is with anybody he feels like. The girl is just there whenever he wants her, but they are not calling it a relationship, it's a continual repeated thing." The serial hookup seems to be the closest synonym students can come up with to dating.

There wasn't a single student who cited a long-term, committed romantic relationship that had emerged from a more traditional dating trajectory, where two people went out on a series of dates to get to know one another over dinner, coffee, or various shared activities like taking walks, going on hikes, watching sporting events, or seeing movies. Students could not cite witnessing this series of events among their friends, either—not because their friends did not want to get into relationships via more traditional dates—but simply because it didn't happen.

Another young man from a secular university was undecided about whether a hookup was a good way into a relationship or not, although he had gotten to the stage of going out with his girlfriend via a serial hookup. On the one hand, a hookup *was* a way of getting to know someone, but on the other hand, maybe it wasn't the *best* way to get to know a person in whom you feel romantic interest. "Maybe kissing is a way to show someone that you're interested in them, or that you like them a lot," he said. "Or, if you just happen to hook up with somebody randomly, then later you find out, Maybe I want to date them. But I think in most cases it's really not [a good way]." This student was happy to be in a committed relationship by the time of our interview, preferring this stage to the one where they had been only hookup partners. "I think everybody has a sexual drive and everybody wants to feel attractive and wants to hook up with other people purely on a physical level. Everybody has that part of them, and I used to indulge in that. But now since I actually found somebody [with] who[m] [hooking up is] not the only thing, I think I can appreciate the other part of the relationship much more, which I think is more important."

One first-year man at a Catholic school tried to explain that it wasn't that *relationships* didn't exist on his campus, but that traditional *dates* didn't exist—at least not until the serial hookup turned into a committed relationship. "For the most part, people hook up beforehand. Normally it starts off as one thing, but it could go to dating." *After* the serial hookup had turned into a long-term, committed relationship, a couple might decide to go to the movies, to dinner, or for a hike.

Another first-year student from a Catholic college, a woman, was fairly descriptive of this process at her school. "A lot of the kids start being really close friends. Then they get drunk and you see them being more together than apart."

A senior at a secular university theorized that even though dating was uncommon at her school, it wasn't that people didn't want to date, it was just that dating in a traditional sense was not available on their campus. "The majority of the time, I do believe that the goal is to eventually date someone," she said. "But I feel like in the meantime, people will just hook up until they find the person they want to date."

Many students can recount the love stories of their parents. One sophomore at a Catholic school claimed that it was "more common for people to be single" on her campus, yet also spoke wistfully about how her parents met and fell in love during college. On one family trip to visit her parents' alma mater, the parents took their kids on a tour of their romance's most significant moments and favorite spots for dates. "I thought in high school that [we got] immature relationships out of the way, and if you wanted to have a relationship in college, then it was going to be serious, because you hear about my generation's parents who met the loves of their life in college, who had this great whirlwind relationship and decided to get married and have kids," she said. "Then I got here and I said, 'Oh my God, it's totally not like that at all.'"

This should make us wonder what will happen when the children of hookup culture become the parents sending their kids off to college. Many will have only the story of hooking up to tell. The awareness about what to expect from college in terms of romance (or a lack of it) will have shifted. For now, many students know that, while earlier generations may have had romance, or at least a chance at it, they do not. These students mourn this loss, especially when they are juniors and seniors and their time at college is running out.

When the subject of romance came up, both men and women shared elaborate fantasies of what a romantic encounter would entail for them. They sounded a lot like old-fashioned dates. Out of 99 students who wrote at length about romance, 64 understood romance as primarily talking: talking for hours upon hours, yet doing so in a beautiful setting—with lit candles everywhere or thousands of stars in the sky above their picnic blanket, or with the sound of waves lapping at the shore, or maybe two wine glasses clinking across a table. Any talk of sexual intimacy, even kissing, was virtually absent from their descriptions. An additional 14 students had similar accounts of romance, understanding it as an opportunity for communication and connection, but also included kissing as part of the equation. Overall, students spoke of romance in a way that seemed utterly distinct, even the opposite of the type of interaction fostered by a hookup. If a hookup is about being sexually active while remaining noncommunicative and disconnected, then romance is the opposite: it's about talking, connecting, and being intimately known by another person.[1]

Many students also felt embarrassed about their romantic yearnings, especially men. Their fantasies about romance often remained unfulfilled wishes for them while on campus. Students believed they were living in a time when they should no longer need such gestures and symbols. They had gotten the message that they should be beyond romance, having been "liberated" from such traditional expectations and hopes. Hookup culture has taught college students that they should skip the romance and go straight to sex.

Yet, on a personal level, most of these same students didn't want to be thought of merely as someone to have sex with after a night of drunken partying, or someone to walk away from without a care. Men and women both spoke of how they wanted to be made to feel special, to experience what it was like when someone else wanted to know everything about them. They yearned for someone to make an effort to create a beautiful setting in which such knowing and being known could occur, for someone who would set aside lavish amounts of time for this to take place. That women and men harbor secret wishes for what appear to be the old-fashioned trappings of romance seems symptomatic of hookup culture's failings. What they want is everything that hookup culture leaves out. The hookup is not liberating at all if what young men and women really want is to go out on dates.

THE TYPICAL PROGRAMMING on campus around the subject of sex, while important, can indirectly reinforce the notion that college students don't date. The basic framework that most institutions use for educating college students about sex, at both Catholic and secular universities, is laid out during the first-year orientation. It deals with the how-to's of protecting yourself from STIs and pregnancy as well as preventing sexual assault. These are the "Sex Rules," if you will. Some words of wisdom about good sex are thrown in, sometimes at length, and often these words of wisdom contain good relationship advice.[2] These are important lessons, yet they are insufficient. For all the good the orientation designers have in mind, they also end up reinforcing three problematic perceptions common within hookup culture:

1. Sex is dangerous.

2. Everyone assumes at college you will be regularly having sex.

3. People don't date here.

The last message, even though it isn't intended, is implicit. The orientation sex talks, though they are sex-positive and dispense important information, happen only once and often last for only an hour, and the entire program typically revolves around the subject of sex. Omission becomes a powerful method of indirectly reinforcing the notion that everything is about having sex at this college and hooking up is the norm. These onetime talks are not enough to prepare college first-years (or sophomores, juniors, and seniors, for that matter) for the realities of hookup culture. Even more significant, they do not empower students to assert their personal values about dating and romance. The fact that colleges tend to sponsor programming only around the rules of sex and not, for instance, around dating neglects this potential aspect of a student's social life, reinforcing the idea that dating doesn't matter at college.

We need to stop assuming that teens and young adults know how to date; that they understand how to approach a person to whom they are attracted; that they have the skills to say, "Let's go get coffee," or "Would you be interested in having dinner sometime?"; that they know how to plan a date, where to go, what to do on one, who pays, and when a kiss goodnight is appropriate, especially if they are not drunk; that they are skilled at next steps and conveying genuine interest. Statements like, "You would never just walk up to someone and just start making out with them if you weren't intoxicated,"[3] reveal a common theme among many students interviewed for the study—a lack of understanding about how to create circumstances to express romantic feeling outside of a drunken party.

College students turn to large amounts of alcohol in order to ease their anxieties about such initial exchanges and intimacies and to cover up for the fact that they lack these basic skills of interaction. The notion of educating teens and young adults about dating and romance may seem frivolous in the face of possible pregnancy and as news about the spread of STIs gets perpetually worse. But failing to pass on the how-to's of communication around basic romantic interest only reinforces such problems and the hookup culture that goes along with them.[4] If teens and young adults are truly to learn to have good, safe sex, then perhaps some attention to dating education beyond the requisite college sex-talks is warranted.

KERRY CRONIN, DIRECTOR of the Lonergan Institute at Boston College, is doing her best to address this gap in education among students at her institution. Cronin has developed a model for dating that pairs in-class discussion with out-of-the-classroom life skills. In the spring of 2005, Cronin gave her students an unusual assignment in a one-credit capstone seminar: to go out on a date. What precipitated this assignment was a conversation with some seniors at BC who had informed her that they had never been on a date at college. She found this so unbelievable that she began polling other students with these three questions: "Are you dating anyone?" "Have you ever?" and "If not, why not?" Cronin quickly learned that students were dying to talk about dating, even though most of them didn't have any dating experience. From these conversations she found out about the dominance of hookup culture on campus and learned that it was keeping students from getting to date.

That same winter, Cronin and two women colleagues held a panel called "Take Back the Date," an event that turned out to be standing-room-only. Cronin and her colleagues had diligently prepared to answer student questions on sexual ethics, moral reasoning, philosophical and theological attitudes about sex, and even the explicit how-to's of sex. But the types of questions from the packed auditorium were far more basic and innocent: "How do you ask someone out?" "Where do you go on a date?" and "Who pays?"

The following semester, Cronin told her eleven seminar students that she wanted them to go out on a date. The assignment was not mandatory at this stage. "They all agreed to do it, and they talked about it *all* semester—the assignment itself, how to ask someone out, etc.," Cronin said. "But in the end and after all that talk, only *one* person—one!—got up the courage to actually go on a date. The rest chickened out. The anxieties they expressed about why ranged from, 'People are going to think I am strange,' to 'I can't think of anybody I would like or would want to ask out.' I kept thinking, *This is a college with 9,000 undergraduates—how many people do you need? You really can't find anyone you'd like to go for coffee with?*"

The inability to act on the desire to go on a date went beyond fear for Cronin's students. Hookup culture was so overwhelming that they couldn't get out from under the "hookup script," as she put it. Dating was so outside the norm that her students had no idea how to set up a date in such an environment. That's when Cronin decided to make the dating assignment mandatory, as it's been ever since.

"At the very beginning of the third semester [that she assigned the date], I stipulated that students could not pass the class unless they did the dating assignment," Cronin said. "By then people were signing up knowing this would be the assignment, and some admitted taking [my] seminar solely because of it—they knew they needed someone to force them to go on a date or they never would."

Today, Cronin's "Go on a Date" assignment has quite a reputation at Boston College. She has developed extensive, written directions over the years to go with it. Not only has the class become more popular with every semester, but "The Date" à la Professor Cronin has acquired a certain aura among undergraduates at BC. Everyone seems to know about it, even students who have not been in the class. "By the fifth or sixth semester [that I taught the class], there wasn't anyone on campus who hadn't heard of the assignment," said Cronin. "Eventually people who weren't even in the seminar started to do it, too. People started telling me how they really relied on the assignment to justify asking someone out. It was typical for [students] to actually mention they were required to go on a date for a class while asking the person out. Because so many people on campus already knew about it, it was that much easier to do the asking."

During one semester, Cronin recalled, a young man became invested in how to make the asking-out part of the assignment more manageable and authentic, so he came up with phrasing to accommodate both needs and shared it with his peers: "I have this assignment to go out on a date, but I've been wanting to ask you out for a long time anyway." This allowed students to use the assignment as a crutch and as a legitimate invitation to go on a date.

But asking someone out isn't the only struggle Cronin's students have faced. Over the years, she has tweaked her assignment sheet by adding a few requirements to make the dating experience more "legitimate." Highlights in the assignment include:

- You must ask someone out in person (i.e., not in a text message, Facebook, or IM).

- This person must be someone who is a legitimate romantic interest (i.e., not just a friend).

- Do not go to a movie on the first date. A movie is at odds with the aim of a first date, which is to get to know the other person through conversation.

- The date may be a daytime or nighttime date, but the date must occur before 10:00 p.m. A walk around the reservoir at midnight or later is not a date, it's sketchy. Or it's the beginning of a hookup.

- The date must involve no alcohol.

Cronin's assignment is the same whether students are men or women, gay or straight. It includes advice on planning at least "three or four" questions to possibly ask the person they are dating ahead of time. In addition, a date only counts if it's two people (no third wheels or double-dating). She also provides examples of what to say at the end of the date if it was enjoyable and the student would like to go out on another date with this person. Instructions for how to be polite about ending a date when a second one is not on the horizon are also included. One of the most crucial requirements, in Cronin's opinion, was sparked by what she had learned about the nature of hookup culture: "There shall be no physical interaction during the date," the assignment says, "with the possible exception of a friendly 'A-Frame' hug at the end."[5]

The assignment particulars have evolved over the past few years. Early on, Cronin realized that her students were cheating: they were asking friends out on dates as a way of avoiding the risk of asking someone who was a legitimate romantic interest. So she added a clause about this to the assignment sheet. But the rule with the most significant impact on the students' experiences was the one related to gossip: how many people students may tell about the date. Cronin allows her students a paltry three friends in whom they can confide. "Before I added this rule," she said,

> the students would tell everyone they knew about the assignment—85 of their closest friends, and then those friends would tell 100 more people, and suddenly 185 people are offering advice and opinions about who the student should ask—or not. People start to live vicariously through your date, and so many people become invested that it can become paralyzing. Especially with my students' heterosexual women friends, everyone begins to weigh in on the guy you've chosen, how they know him, what he was like freshman year, and who he's hooked up with. It becomes a big drama.

Now that Cronin limits the gossip to three friends only, almost all of her students claim that keeping the date to themselves is *the* most important rule.

One of Cronin's more controversial rules is the one that says, if you ask, you pay. Cronin tells her students that the first date is reconnaissance, that you are setting up a circumstance in which you can get to know a potential partner better and do some information gathering. One of the ways to put your best foot forward is to pay. This shows that you are generous, that you are invested, and that you care enough about the experience that you are literally investing in it. Women tend to have a much more difficult time with this rule than men, but Cronin reminds her students that if the date goes well and leads to something more, then they can take turns paying on future dates.

After teaching this class for a number of semesters, Cronin has come to believe that teens and young adults today simply have no dating practices, dating habits, or basic interpersonal skills applicable to dating—with the emphasis on interpersonal as opposed to virtual. This isn't just a case of nerves and hookup culture filling in for an experience students would rather avoid. And the goal is certainly not about helping students get more quickly to sex. Students know little else other than how to drink enough to become sexually intimate with a random partner. As they skip over dating and go straight to sex, they begin to realize not only that something is missing, but that they are missing out on what may be, for them, the most important experience of all that dating provides—the chance to get to know their partner. Somewhere deep down, students suspect that the key to good sex is knowing another person and being known by them *before* sex, and having the chance (or many chances) to sit across from that person, with both partners sober, to ask, "So, what makes you, you?" They simply haven't learned how to make this happen.

Cronin worries that "we" are part of the problem—whether "we" are parents, faculty, staff, or campus administrators—because we haven't taught our children and students the rules of dating or updated the dating scripts of old. "Manners and social scripts give us a comfort level that allows reasonable pacing for getting to know another person, so you know what is expected and when, and what isn't, and you can let yourself go along with the script," Cronin said. "But now, because dating has disappeared, students really have *no idea* what to expect. Students are so in need of guidance and conversation about the loneliness and the pain they feel, and you realize that hookup culture and their inexperience with dating is just this open wound. I stepped into it rather by accident, having no idea at first the extent of it, and suddenly there it was: this level of desire and need on their part. I can't believe how little I'd paid attention to it beforehand."

Meanwhile, teens and young adults sit in silence, assuming they are the only people who feel this way, who want these things. "You are not supposed to admit that hookups hurt your feelings and make you lonely," said Cronin. "You shouldn't even admit this to yourself, they think. You should just stop being needy and get over it, because hooking up is supposed to be fun and you should party at college. That's what everybody wants and does."

Cronin has found that, while faculty and staff are dumbfounded by the ways hookup culture dominates campus life and students' sexual decision-making, they are also paralyzed about what to do in response. Sometimes they are disdainful about promoting dating as an antidote to hookup culture. "I have gotten pushback from faculty who will tell me that I'm encouraging young women to participate in patriarchal structures that are based on the buying and selling of women," she said. "But hookup culture is oppressive of everyone. Where is the feminist outcry about it?'

In its ideal form, feminism is about giving voice and empowerment to everyone and not letting people feel marginalized, oppressed, or used. It is about calling out oppression no matter where it shows up. "Hookup culture is all about the commodification of myself; buying and selling myself to make myself less lonely, while at the same time making myself lonelier in the process," Cronin said. "It's such a capitalist structure." The sad part of this, for Cronin, is the way that campus pushback leaves students to struggle with these issues on their own, without the resources to respond to their situation in ways that are direct, practical, and empowering. "You are only about three or four questions away from finding your students' pain, and most likely only *one* good question."

NOT EVERY FACULTY MEMBER on a college campus has to give out dating assignments. Nor does every student affairs staff member or university administrator need to appear on panels, or plan and run programs giving students alternatives to hookup culture. But we are responsible for knowing who will do such things. That way, when the wounded begin to appear, people on campus will be aware which faculty member, staffperson, or administrator will be able to have that deeper conversation about these subjects that are so important to students' lives.

Talk of dating how-to's might seem frivolous at first glance, and it would be easy to write off arguments to "bring back the date" as a nostalgic response to hookup culture by an older generation that liked their way better, as Hannah Rosin did in "Boys on the Side," her 2012 article in *The Atlantic*.[6] But dismissing the date outright betrays a failure of imagination in the same way liberals and moderates have written off abstinence: What about *re*imagining the structure and purpose of the date for a generation that relates to gender differently? Many students are struggling within hookup culture. It has many degrading gender implications and can act as a coercive force in students' social lives. It can be debilitating to students and to the development of their sexual identities and sexual decision-making skills. Given all these problems with hookup culture, the possibility of dating as an alternative to it begins to take on new significance.

Dating lessons could offer students a way of approaching one another on a less explicit, less alcohol-soaked, less high-risk, and more nuanced, engaged level. The most basic idea behind a date is that two people who find each other attractive are carving out time to sit down face to face and get to know each other. The face-to-faceness of the practice forces us to contend with the very fact of their humanity and combats the treatment of the other as object in our world of new technology. What's more, to reckon with someone's personhood in this way has the potential to devastate hookup culture and its teaching that we should no longer acknowledge such things as the basic human value of the person with whom we might someday (or later that night) share a bed. Shifting the attitude on campus from *no one ever dates here* to, at the very least, *some people do date here*, could lead to more students experiencing sex that is good, empowering, pleasurable, connective, and constructive to their self-esteem and relationships with others down the road.

A New Kind of Sex Education:
Good Sex 101 and Critical Living Skills

LATELY, EVERY TIME I SPEAK ABOUT my study and my book *Sex and the Soul,* people ask me if I have seen the HBO series *Girls.* The show has been hailed as this generation's *Sex and the City* because it's about sex and the single girl, and yet it lacks the glamour and sexiness that Carrie, Samantha, Charlotte, and Miranda brought to their adventures as best friends living it up in New York City.

In an op-ed column in the *New York Times,* journalist Frank Bruni expressed his perplexity about what the series seemed to be saying about the younger generation—in particular its women—and their relationship to sex. He described how, during sex scenes, the women characters seemed present more as "props," to be told dispassionately to move this way or that for the purpose of male pleasure, than as "partners." The women's roles were to be "largely a fleshy canvas" for male fantasies during sex. "You watch these scenes," Bruni wrote, "and other examples

179

of the zeitgeist-y, early-20s heroines of 'Girls' engaging in, re-
coiling from, mulling and mourning sex, and you think: Gloria
Steinem went to the barricades for *this*? Salaries may be better
than in decades past and the cabinet and Congress less choked
with testosterone. But in the bedroom? What's happening there
remains something of a muddle, if not something of a mess."[1]

Watching the sex scenes of this series is like watching
hookup culture come to life, as though the stories of the thousands of students with whom I have spoken over the past few
years were pulled together and made into a television show.
The pilot's sex scene has the main character heading to the
apartment of what appears to be her serial hookup partner,
who, after some jokes that she should be his sex slave, begins
giving her directions in a monotone voice about what he wants
her to do—lay face down on the couch, bend her knees, remove
her skirt and stockings so she's naked from the waist down.
When she becomes uneasy about his plans to have anal sex, he
agrees to simply have sex with her from behind—at which
point they make distracted small talk, until eventually he re-
quests they shift to "quiet time." There is an element of humor
built into everyone's ambivalence toward just about every aspect
of their post-college lives, yet ultimately it is difficult to find
such depressing ambivalence funny.

It has been difficult enough to listen to so much sadness
about the state of college sex, but to see it on screen is a new
level of disheartening. It fairly begs viewers to ask: is this what
we want for the next generation with respect to sex? I've long

wondered what the post-college, twenty-something, professional world would look like as the hookup generation graduated from college, and the HBO series *Girls* appears determined to portray exactly this. To compare the show to *Sex and the City* seems strange—not only does *Girls* lack the glamour and sexiness of this earlier HBO hit, but *Girls* also lacks the playfulness and camaraderie of the earlier show's four famous characters. This new series about "girls" seems to turn on the notion that everything about post-college life is ambivalent; that there is little to which anyone today might aspire. That the sex is depressing and boring, too, is par for the course.

RECENTLY AT A UNIVERSITY LECTURE, a young woman in the audience asked me—in all sincerity—why sex was such a big deal. "Why does sex have to be any different than, say, taking a walk by myself?" she wondered. "What distinguishes sex from all the other things we do that *aren't* such a big deal?" A number of students began to speculate in answer. They definitely thought that sex was a big deal, though no one could articulate why they felt this way.

In response to their discussion, I suggested we consider the meaning of sex and talk about what they thought good sex was. It was soon clear that these students had never pondered such topics. Questions came up like the following: What would good sex feel like? Who would it be with? In what kind of setting? Would it be brief and casual? Would they want to have sex with some form of commitment, and if so, why? If not, why not? Such questions were foreign to their university experience. It was a struggle for them to imagine what good sex might entail. It was as though, until that moment, it had not occurred to anyone that they not only had the right to ask such questions, but owed it to themselves to do so if they were thinking of having or already having sex. Not only hookup culture, but American popular culture and the politics of the left and the right had taught these students that sex was something defined *for* them and not *by* them. Despite being at college—a place where critical thinking about the social and political spheres is expected to occur—these students had never weighed in on the meaning of sex, or been empowered to realize that, in fact, it is their *right* to define what they want out of sex.

The great irony of hookup culture—whether pre-, during, or post-college—is that it's ultimately a culture of repression. If the Victorian era represents the repression of sexual desire, then the era of the hookup is about the repression of romantic feeling, love, and sexual desire, too, in favor of greater access to sex—sex for the sake of sex. Women and men both learn to shove their desires deep down into a dark place, to be revealed to no one. They learn to be ashamed if they long for love, and embarrassed if they fail to uphold the social contract of hookup culture and do not happen to enjoy no-strings-attached sex that much.

The further irony of hookup culture is that, while being sexually active is the norm for students, the sex itself becomes mechanical as a result of so much repression of emotion. College, ideally, is supposed to function as a time in life when young people get to let go of repression; it's supposed to open them up to the world, not shut them down to it; it's supposed to encourage them to become who they are meant to become, not teach them to hide that self; and, most of all, college is supposed to empower them to find their voices and speak up, not learn that the voices bubbling up inside of them are shameful. That a culture that has come to dominate so many colleges and universities thwarts these ideals among its students—and within an aspect of their lives that is so central, intimate, and identity-shaping as sex—is unacceptable.

Another question I am often asked at lectures is some variation of "Who is to blame for hookup culture?" There are the obvious speculations that follow—the cultural obsession with celebrity and pop stars, television and the movies, technology, and the fact that today pornography is ubiquitous. While all of these have contributed to the existence of hookup culture, we also must consider the role that colleges themselves play in its perpetuation. Colleges are supposed to be centers of intellectual inquiry, of cultural critique and evaluation, places where community members—faculty, staff, administration, and students alike—enter into dialogue about the world around them. Therefore, colleges should be the very locations where something like hookup culture could not survive. Instead, colleges are producing all of the following:

- Women's studies majors to whom it does not occur that there might be a disconnect between their work in the history of the feminist movement and the fact that they attend theme parties on the weekend

- Male students who do not seem to know that they are struggling to live up to gendered expectations that may not suit them, or are afraid to admit they might be, since that somehow might cost them their masculinity

- Women and men who learn to hide their true opinions and any aspects of themselves that might mark them as outside the norm, despite the fact that their colleges boast communities of tolerance

- Students who learn to be ashamed of their politics

- Young men who engage in the stereotypical male bravado expected by college "guys" in American culture, while burying all emotion and vulnerability

- A generation that is more socially activist than ever, yet whose members have no idea how to apply the ideals of social justice to their own actions and immediate community or how to foster an awareness of human dignity at their parties and in their sexual decision-making

It is well known that much of a college education takes place outside the classroom, yet many colleges falter in their effort to empower students to apply what they learn in their courses to life beyond those four walls. Faculty members are trained in an academy that devalues the personal as a valid source of inquiry, reflection, and application; that teaches aspiring PhDs that to relate their own work or a classroom conversation to personal subjects (like sex and relationships) is to strip away the rigor required for research; that to open the subject one studies and teaches to the lives of the very real bodies that fill their classrooms is to somehow water everything down. Yet, to bracket the personal is to undermine a college community's ability to respond to the culture of hooking up in which their students live, socialize, and have sex. That students are rarely empowered to bring their critical-thinking skills to bear on their own lives within the college classroom should give everyone pause.

An effective response to hookup culture could be as simple as inviting students to apply critical-thinking skills to the task of evaluating their weekend activities; asking them to draw on their on-campus experiences as they discuss gender, politics, philosophy, literature, theology, education, and social justice inside the classroom; teaching them that their experiences are valid sources for evaluation; allowing the personal to be of value; and making sure students understand that the "I"—a personal pronoun many professors still teach does not belong in student papers—is imperative if they are to understand their role as subjects in relation to their studies. Helping students make this connection between critical thinking and critical living is the best method for tackling the negatives of hookup culture. Encouraging this kind of thinking (and living) recognizes that, at its root, hookup culture silences, shames, isolates, and disempowers students, quashing their ethics, desires, and differences, their need for respect and connection, and their need to be treated with bodily dignity, to express emotion, and to experience pleasure. To get beyond the "whateverism" that hookup culture breeds among those living within it, students must be empowered to put those critical-thinking skills to work, evaluating hookup culture itself as a college "text" in its own right, a text that is relevant to studies that consider gender, sexual orientation, politics, moral and religious commitments, and many of the other topics that so many of their classes examine.

The tools for addressing such issues are embedded in the loftiest texts of the Western canon itself, in classics like Plato's *The Symposium* and Aristotle's *Nicomachean Ethics*, in St. Augustine's *Confessions*, and in Shakespeare's plays and sonnets. A text like Descartes's *Meditations* could help communities raise questions about how new technologies affect our ideas of sex and our experience of the body. In the spirit of Socrates, many college administrations, faculty, and staff already love to challenge students to think about queries such as Who am I? What does it mean to be human? Do I have a purpose? What is the good? The true? as they navigate through a core curriculum and a variety of majors. All a university needs to do is expressly open up texts like these to classroom conversations about the meaning (or lack thereof) of sex within the college experience, about relationships, and about how students treat one another and behave on the weekends.

The good news about discussing good sex in the midst of hookup culture is that all the potential conditions exist in the courses already taught and in the structures already in place for programming on a college campus. Applying these resources to this particular conversation must be an intentional and co-ordinated effort, however, and it requires an awareness among faculty, staff, and college administrators about the issues surrounding sex and hooking up on campus. We need to acknowledge that the subject of "good sex" is important to the college experience, and in fact just as important as any other subject when it comes to preparing the students of today to make their way in the world as the confident, empowered, respectful citizens we hope they turn out to be. I would go so far as to say that colleges and universities need to think about where the topic of educating their students about good sex fits into those mission statements I spoke about in this book's Introduction, since the attitudes students develop about sex are a central part of who they become by the time they graduate.

For this dialogue to be successful, there must also be an openness about the fact that "good sex" may ultimately mean different things to different people. It could include hooking up, long-term love, romance, dating, saving sex for a later date (be that next semester or for marriage), or taking a "time-out" from sex for a while. Students need time for personal (and academic) reflection to figure out what this meaning is for them In this space for reflection, there is so much for students to consider: the circumstances in which sex occurs; the timing of sex; the type of relationship (if any) in place before sex occurs; the many kinds of sexual intimacy that are possible; whether they would like to be "in love," or "in like," or simply attracted to a partner; what role their emotions play, and what role their partner's emotions play; the ways in which they might experience pleasure and also give pleasure to their partner; what happens after the sex. The possibilities of how someone might decide what good sex looks like are vast. If colleges and universities include study and reflection on sex and relationship as part of their mission—given hookup culture on campus— they will be helping students open their eyes and see that the hookup is just one option among many for navigating sexuality and romantic relationship during their young-adult lives, and that, most of all, it is their right to choose which option is best. When they are ready.

Acknowledgments

Writing this follow up to *Sex and the Soul* has been a long journey, and I would like to thank Lara Heimert, my editor with the endless patience, and also Elizabeth Stein and Katherine Streckfus for their amazing editorial expertise. I am also grateful to all the generous staff at Basic, especially Katy O'Donnell and Rachel King. Nothing would ever get done in my writing life without the support of my wonderful agent Miriam Altshuler, who I am lucky enough to have worked with for almost a decade now. A special thanks also goes out to Iza Wojciechowska who provided me with both excellent research assistance and great company while she was finishing her MFA at Columbia. Then, of course, this project would not exist without the thousands of students all over the United States who have spoken with me over the years about their college experiences—both for the formal study and during lecture visits—as well as the colleges and universities who have hosted me. I thank you, most of all, for your generosity.

On the Practical:
Concrete Ways to Respond
to Hookup Culture

Young adults move through various communities as they grow up; besides the home, these communities include their schools and colleges. In each, the programming and education around sex must be expanded in creative ways. Young people today need dating education, love-story education, relationship education, and a new kind of abstinence education. If we want to empower them to escape the hookup culture in which they now find themselves, we need to instruct them in the techniques of romance.

Things Parents Can Do

- Talk about how you fell in love. Tell your kids the story, from the first moment you saw each other to how you ended up deciding to date, and so on.

- Many people have been in love multiple times: recount these stories as well, from beginning to end.

- Teach your kids tips for dating, including how to ask someone out. Give them pointers about what to say to a person they like.

- Talk about romance with your kids: What are some of the most romantic things you've ever experienced? Romantic places you've gone to? Ask your kids about what they long for in terms of romance.

- When your kids approach the college search age, let dating, romance, and love be part of the conversation when deciding what they want out of college. Do your kids hope to fall in love while at college? If so, are the colleges you are looking at good places to foster relationships, or is hookup culture the only culture on campus?

Parents and college applicants alike today will have to face the reality that it is difficult to find campus atmospheres that actively promote dating and relationships as opposed to hookup culture. But if parents and applicants begin to prioritize a dating/relationship culture in the college search, college admissions officers will be put in a position where they will have to begin answering questions about how their campuses are responding to hookup culture. This may lead them to begin offering alternative models as well as discussion and programming centering on how to enter into relationships while at college.

Things Administrators and Staff Members Can Do

- During admissions tours and conversations, address the dating climate on campus.

- During freshman orientation, have juniors and seniors who are helping out give talks on their favorite dates and most romantic evenings. Consider sponsoring a Top Ten Romantic Spots on Campus Tour, or a Top Ten Best Places to Take a Date Tour.

- Sponsor a panel on Dating Tips and Etiquette.

- Sponsor a program called "Can We Kiss?" that is actually about how to get that first kiss and *not* about sexual assault.

- Foster programs where students have to go on a date, like "Date Night" at the on-campus coffee shop, and include a gift card for two coffees so students don't have to worry about cost.

- Take advantage of the growing population of students who do volunteer and social justice work on campus, empowering them to take social justice ideals and apply them to their after-dark and weekend partying activities.

Even if a campus does not have a vibrant dating culture, an easy way to create one is to simply talk about how dating *can* be a part of campus life. Convey the message that "it's okay to date here." Junior and senior students have the most influence and authority over campus culture and are the best resources for giving first-year students permission to date and for modeling dating practices in general for other students.

Setting up programs during fall and spring semesters where administration, staff, and faculty members sponsor a panel or talk to handle questions and offer tips on dating and relationships can be fun for both students and panelists. Students get to hear advice about dating from people they know and respect on campus. Again, this reinforces the idea that hookup culture is not the only option. Sponsoring playful, fun, lighthearted programs around the less explicit side of sex (kissing, for example) reinforces for students that it's okay to think about the wide range of forms of sexual intimacy. Giving students permission to be a little more innocent with their sex lives is an effective and simple response to hookup culture.

Things Faculty Members Can Do

- Consider what course materials and readings already assigned on your syllabi would lend themselves to discussions about dating, romance, love, sex, and hooking up in ways that students can relate to personally.

- Develop questions in response to this material that will send students off thinking about how to apply the course material to their personal lives and weekend activities.

- If questions arise in response to course material from students that involve their personal experiences, affirm that this sort of connection is welcome in classroom discussion, but also require them to root their comments in the text rather than go astray on a tangent.

- More ambitious faculty members may consider developing a section of a course or an entire course tackling these topics.

- Those willing to experiment may consider coming up with creative assignments. (For example, require students to go out on a date (see Chapter 8), or have them attempt to follow Aristotle's "mean" during all of their weekend activities and report back.)

The disciplines of literature, philosophy, theology, history, education, and psychology most easily lend themselves to entire courses on such topics. Students will flock to courses like "The History of Dating," "The Philosophy of Love," "The Psychology of Relationships," or "Romance in British [and/or American] Literature." They are dying for classroom opportunities to discuss these things and eager to invest in their work and readings at a high intellectual level in this sort of course. Many students yearn for mature, rigorous conversation about these topics. It is important that faculty encourage students to question the standards and practices of hookup culture, just as they would with any other power structure or cultural construct. This empowers students to consider alternatives to hooking up that they could enact in their own lives, as well as the meaning and purpose of sex according to them.

Tackling hookup culture via the college curriculum can be fairly simple. The material necessary is already embedded across the course catalog. Even if a faculty member devotes twenty minutes here and there during a class three or four times a semester—or even one single class—this can be useful. Sometimes all it takes is sending students off with a question to think about when class is over—"What do you think Aristotle would say about the party you are about to attend tonight, given the reading? Consider it and we'll discuss on Monday." If a professor is already teaching love poetry, why not open up the discussion for a bit to talk about whether this type of love-speak is familiar in the students' own lives. Or, if a professor is teaching the tradition of letter writing, say, between Abelard and Heloise, ask students if they have ever written or received a love letter, and if so, in what context? Related assignments could include writing someone a love letter in the vein of a particular author or tradition. During the following class, the professor could encourage students to evaluate their work in light of the genre. These sorts of assignments can lend themselves to lively student discussions. The students would not only be learning more about the course material, but practicing it, both as writers and as real people with hearts who love and long to express that love.

All it takes is for a faculty member to be willing to be a little creative. Faculty members who take the time to allow students to make these connections between their studies and their lives—to put this little twist on something they already teach—can make all the difference for young people who are struggling with hookup culture and seeking a more authentic way of approaching relationships and social life.

Notes

Introduction: The Second Shift of College

1. The best chance at a thorough sociological look at hooking up is with Christian Smith's longitudinal National Study of Youth and Religion (NSYR), which began in 2001 and is tracking the religious affinities of American youth from age thirteen into their early thirties. Although Smith is interested primarily in religious attitudes, he is also gathering wider data on his participants' lives, including information on sexuality and sexual decision-making. The list of articles and books Smith has published with his fellow researchers and graduate students on behalf of the NSYR is impressive. It includes Christian Smith and Melinda Lundquist, *Soul Searching: The Religious Lives of American Teenagers* (New York: Oxford University Press, 2005), and Christian Smith and Patricia Snell, *Souls in Transition: The Religious and Spiritual Lives of Emerging Adults* (New York: Oxford University Press, 2009). See also Kenda Creasy Dean, *Almost Christian: What the Faith of*

Our Teenagers Is Telling the American Church (New York: Oxford University Press, 2010), and Mark Regnerus, *Forbidden Fruit: Sex and Religion in the Lives of American Teenagers* (New York: Oxford University Press, 2007). But the portrait this research will produce of American youth, including the effects and shifts of hookup culture on young adults over time, remains to be seen. Even when the study is complete, it will only trace hookup culture to 2001, when the origins of the culture date back much further than this.

2. See Laura Sessions Stepp, *Unhooked: How Young Women Pursue Sex, Delay Love, and Lose at Both* (New York: Riverhead, 2007), and Kathleen Bogle, *Hooking Up: Sex, Dating, and Relationships on Campus* (New York: New York University Press, 2008). For Bogle's discussions on the history of the hookup, see Chapters 1 and 2.

3. On the ways in which new technology and social media are not only rewiring our brains, but changing how we relate to others, see the series entitled "Your Brain on Computers," *New York Times*, published on various dates throughout 2010 and indexed at http://topics.nytimes.com/top/features/timestopics/series/your_brain_on_computers/index.html, accessed October 1, 2012.

4. Hanna Rosin, "Boys on the Side," *The Atlantic*, September 2012, www.theatlantic.com/magazine/archive/2012/09/boys-on-the-side/309062/, accessed August 24, 2012. See also Hanna Rosin, *The End of Men: And the Rise of Women* (New York: Riverhead, 2012).

5. See Donna Freitas, *Sex and the Soul: Juggling Sexuality, Spirituality, Romance and Religion on America's College Campuses* (New York: Oxford University Press, 2008), 156–160. More than 700 students from the Catholic, private-secular, and public colleges responded to an open-ended question in the survey about how they perceive their peers' attitudes about sex on campus. I sorted the comments into seven main categories to arrive at the percentages: friends value sex in committed, loving relationships; peers are open-minded about sex; people *say* they value chastity but secretly engage in sexual activities; peers make sex taboo / closed to discussion / peers aren't casual enough about sex; peers are too casual about sex / suspect that people act "carefree" about sex in public but feel otherwise in private; peer attitudes are divided between those who value chastity and those who do not / those who are casual and those who take sex seriously; and sex is personal / not my business to judge others.

6. Of the 2,500 students who took the online survey, 557 chose to answer an open-ended, optional question that asked them to describe how they felt the morning after a hookup. Of the students who answered, 495 (89 percent) were spread evenly across the Catholic, nonreligious private, and public schools, and the following percentages come from those responses. The 41 percent who expressed "dashed hopes" after a hookup reported a wide range of responses, including feeling awkward, used, dirty, empty, regretful, ashamed, alone, miserable, disgusted, duped, or abused. Those who felt more ambivalent about their experiences said their feelings depended on a number of factors, including whether they

were sober or drunk, whether they had been with a friend or someone they didn't know, whether the person with whom they had hooked up was really okay with the lack of commitment, whether they thought the hookup could turn into something more, and whether it was enjoyable for both parties. One hundred and seventy-nine (36 percent) of the students said they "felt fine" after their hookups, and the adjectives they used were very indifferent. When describing how they felt, they used words such as fine, good, nothing, whatever, mostly okay, and happy. A few stated explicitly that they had no regrets. See Freitas, *Sex and the Soul*, 152–156.

Chapter One: Hookup World: The What, the Why, the How, the Classic vs. the Serial

1. See Caitlin Flanagan, "Are You There God? It's Me, Monica," *The Atlantic*, January/February, 2006, www.theatlantic.com/magazine/archive/2006/01/are-you-there-god-its-me-monica/304511/?single_page=true, accessed October 2, 2012. See also Caitlin Flanagan, "Love, Actually: How Girls Reluctantly Endure the Hookup Culture," *The Atlantic*, June 2010, www.theatlantic.com/magazine/archive/2010/06/love-actually/308094/, accessed October 2, 2012.

2. While my earlier book, *Sex and the Soul: Juggling Sexuality, Spirituality, Romance and Religion on America's College Campuses* (New York: Oxford University Press, 2008), provides many students' stories from the interviews I conducted in their entirety, this book focuses more on how their comments about specific

subjects group together to tell us something about the topic of hooking up, though I still quote extensively from their narratives. In this chapter and the ones that follow, their comments have undergone minor editing for readability, with the frequent use of "like," "um," and other verbal stutters edited out. Also, unless otherwise indicated, the students I quote have identified their sexual orientation as heterosexual. I chose not to indicate sexual orientation each time I quote a student unless they identified as gay, lesbian, or bisexual because the majority of students I quote identified as heterosexual.

3. Out of the 1,015 respondents who answered this question, 786 answered yes, that they had had oral, anal, and/or vaginal sex.

4. For example, when *Conversations*, a higher education magazine run by a group of Jesuit priests and distributed at all the Jesuit universities in the United States, chose to do an interview with me about hookup culture on Catholic campuses, one of the first questions the interviewer asked me was: "According to your studies, can you tell us what percentage of students have had sexual intercourse by the time they arrive in college, how often they would have it each year, and how the pattern compares to non-Catholic colleges?" Before answering the question, I called up the editor to say that, in my opinion, such an inquiry wasn't worth responding to. The question itself was misguided—it focused on the wrong issues and betrayed a lack of sensibility about what really mattered in hookup culture. The editor, a Jesuit priest, gave me a wonderful answer: he told me that I should say exactly what was problematic about the question itself, so their readers

would understand that such inquiries do not give us answers about hookup culture and can even be misleading. If Jesuits are asking outdated questions, he explained, then they need to know this. He asked that I use the interview as an opportunity to discuss why worrying about general statistics for sexual activity on campus is not productive. I felt this was a rather forward-thinking response, and in the interview I was able to address the issue of where our conversations about young adults and sex keep falling apart as well as how to shift the conversation to the things that really matter.

5. In fact, in one study about hooking up and the "friends with benefits" phenomenon, 56 percent of participants simply said that these experiences included all types of sexual intimacy. They resisted agreeing to answers that forced them to define the sexual content (for example, "oral sex only," which only 2.7 percent of participants marked; "intercourse only" [22.7 percent]; or "all but intercourse" [8 percent]). Melissa A. Bisson and Timothy R. Levine, "Negotiating a Friends with Benefits Relationship," *Archives of Sexual Behavior* 38, no. 1 (2009).

Chapter Two: The All-Purpose Alcohol Solution

1. Donna E. Howard, Melinda A. Griffin, and Bradley O. Boekeloo, "Prevalence and Psychosocial Correlates of Alcohol-Related Sexual Assault Among University Students," *Adolescence* 43 (2008).

2. Jennifer L. Brown and Peter A. Vanable, "Alcohol Use, Partner Type, and Risky Sexual Behavior Among College

Students: Findings from an Event-Level Study." *Addictive Behaviors* 32, no. 12 (2007): 2940–2952. See also William F. Flack Jr., Marcia L. Caron, Sarah J. Leinen, Katherine G. Breitenbach, Ann M. Barber, Elaine N. Brown, et al., "'The Red Zone': Temporal Risk for Unwanted Sex Among College Students," *Journal of Interpersonal Violence* 23, no. 9 (2008).

3. Donna Freitas, *Sex and the Soul: Juggling Sexuality, Spirituality, Romance and Religion on America's College Campuses* (New York: Oxford University Press, 2008), 75–92, 113–125.

4. For more discussion of this tendency, see also Brown et al., "Alcohol Use, Partner Type."

5. William F. Flack Jr., Kimberly Daubman, and Marcia Caron, "Risk Factors and Consequences of Unwanted Sex Among University Students: Hooking Up, Alcohol, and Stress Response," *Journal of Interpersonal Violence* 22, no. 2 (2007): 139–157.

6. Flack et al., "'The Red Zone.'"

7. For more discussion of how sexual assault was a factor in student responses for the study, see Freitas, *Sex and the Soul,* 8–9, 149–152.

8. See US Department of Education, "Title IX Enforcement Highlights: Office for Civil Rights," April 4, 2011, www.white house.gov/sites/default/files/dear_colleague_sexual_violence.pdf, accessed April 14, 2012. For information on Title IX's policies with respect to sexual assault on campus, see "Know Your Rights: Title IX Prohibits Sexual Harassment and Sexual Violence Where You Go to School," n.d., www.whitehouse.gov/sites/default/files/fact_sheet_know_your_rights.pdf, accessed April 14, 2012.

Chapter Three: Opting In to a Culture of Casual Sex

1. At public universities and private-secular and Catholic universities, I found that students' attitudes and ideas about how their peers feel about sex and hookup culture varies drastically. At secular schools (both public and private), 42 percent of the students said they thought that their peers were open-minded about sex, and 36 percent said that their peers were too casual in their attitudes about sex. At Catholic universities, the numbers were similar, with 35 percent thinking that their peers were open-minded about sex, and 45 percent thinking that their peers were too casual about sex. At both types of schools, 0 percent said they thought their peers valued chastity openly, or even valued chastity but secretly engaged in sexual activities. See Donna Freitas, *Sex and the Soul: Juggling Sexuality, Spirituality, Romance and Religion on America's College Campuses* (New York: Oxford University Press, 2008), 156–157.

2. According to my data, 45 percent of students at Catholic schools and 36 percent of students at nonreligious private and public schools said that they felt their peers had casual attitudes about sex, but that they had problems with these attitudes. This group said that students on campus "put overwhelming, unwarranted emphasis on sex" and that they were "*too* casual," "careless," and even "hurtful" in this regard. They added that hookup culture makes people "treat sex like a game," or that "campus is like a sex market [where] people are just walking around trying to impress each other and trying to find people to sleep with." Students in this group also thought that their peers' carefree attitudes toward

sex were public façades, and that in private they might be more conservative about their sexual attitudes than it appeared they were. In reality, few students expressed a desire to hook up randomly on a regular basis. See Freitas, *Sex and the Soul*, 157.

Chapter Four: Learning to Play the Part (of Porn Star): The Sexualization of College Girls

1. A discussion of theme parties also appears in Donna Freitas, *Sex and the Soul: Juggling Sexuality, Spirituality, Romance and Religion on America's College Campuses* (New York: Oxford University Press, 2008), 5, 144–148.

2. See Sandra Schneiders, *Women and the Word: The Gender of God in the New Testament and the Spirituality of Women*, Madaleva Lecture in Spirituality (New York: Paulist Press, 1986), 28. Schneiders said that "if God is male, then males are divine and masculinity becomes normative of humanity," but argued that God and "the Father" and "Son" were only metaphorically male, and ignoring a female approach to God may lead to a dangerous, or incomplete, understanding.

3. Pamela Paul, *Pornified: How Pornography Is Transforming Our Loves, Our Relationships, and Our Families* (New York: Times Books, 2005).

4. Ariel Levy, *Female Chauvinist Pigs: Women and the Rise of Raunch Culture* (New York: Free Press, 2005). Levy tags along with *Girls Gone Wild* crews in Miami. Wearing GGW hats and T-shirts, the men are constantly approached by girls willing to flash them or strip completely, make out with each other, masturbate on

camera, or mime sex acts on each other—all for a piece of GGW paraphernalia. Levy argued that the things feminists used to reject—*Playboy*, pornography, debasement—are now being embraced by young women as reclamations of their sexuality and as empowerment. The current accepted wisdom, she wrote, is that "the only alternative to enjoying *Playboy* (or flashing for *Girls Gone Wild* or getting implants or reading Jenna Jameson's memoir) is being 'uncomfortable' with and 'embarrassed' about your sexuality. Raunch culture, then, isn't an entertainment option, it's a litmus test of female uptightness" (40). To listen to Levy's NPR *Fresh Air* interview by Terry Gross, see "Women in the 'Girls Gone Wild' Era," November 28, 2006, www.npr.org/templates/story/story.php ?storyId=6549015, accessed April 4, 2011.

5. *New York Magazine* devoted its entire issue of February 7, 2011, to the topic of how pornography is changing attitudes about sex, how we experience desire, how porn is affecting girls' understanding of sexiness, how girls are learning to use porn and porn archetypes to impress boys, and the role of the Internet in all of this. See Alex Morris, "They Know What Boys Want," *New York Magazine*, February 7, 2011, 32–37. See also Davy Rothbart, "He's Just Not Into Anyone," *New York Magazine*, January 30, 2011, http://nymag.com/news/features/70976/, accessed October 1, 2012.

6. Peggy Orenstein, "Playing at Sexy," *New York Times Magazine*, June 11, 2010.

7. See Stephen Hinshaw and Rachel Kranz, *The Triple Bind: Saving Our Teenage Girls from Today's Pressures* (New York: Ballantine Books, 2009).

8. See Sharon Lamb and Lyn Mikel Brown, *Packaging Girl-hood: Rescuing Our Daughters from Marketers' Schemes* (New York: St. Martin's Griffin, 2006), 1–3, 9, 22–23. Lamb and Brown also observed: "Even Wonder Woman, a rare exception, only '*encourages* fortitude and self-confidence.' That she does so in a spaghetti-strapped leotard with beige stretch nylons and what resembles a bikini bottom suggests the only things she's ready to battle are Halloween-night goose bumps."

Chapter Five: Why We Get Boys Wrong: The Emotional Glass Ceiling

1. See Susannah Meadows, "Sex, Lies & Duke," *Newsweek*, May 1, 2006; Michael Levenson and Jenna Russell, "Milton Academy Rocked by Expulsions," *Boston Globe*, February 20, 2005; Maureen Dowd, "Their Dangerous Swagger," *New York Times*, June 8, 2010.

2. Several of Judd Apatow's popular movies show sex, male and female roles, and relationships through a particular lens that has become embedded in our culture partly because of these movies. In *Forgetting Sarah Marshall* (2008), the protagonist breaks up with his overly demanding girlfriend, is tormented by thoughts of her, and eventually begins to date a nicer, better girl who understands him. *Superbad* (2007) portrays high-school misfits (all boys) who get invited to the cool girls' party by promising to bring alcohol. Most of the movie traces their attempts to get beer (they are underage so it's not easy) and their adolescent anticipation of hooking up with the girls. Once at the party, each of them hooks

up, or tries to, with the girl of his dreams. In *Knocked Up* (2007), the unemployed, sloppy, not-quite-grown-up protagonist has a drunken one-night stand with a woman out of his league (followed by awe and cheering-on by his equally worthless friends). When she becomes pregnant as a result and decides to keep the baby, he is forced to grow up and contribute to the relationship. *Anchorman: The Legend of Ron Burgundy* (2004) is supposed to portray the context of male-dominated 1970s culture, but it involves the protagonist drunkenly hitting on women, sexist and arrogant seduction attempts, and the protagonist's boasts about sleeping with the female character.

3. See Leslie Bennetts, "Heigl's Anatomy," *Vanity Fair*, January 2008. Judd Apatow's reaction in the article to Heigl's comments is in line with the attitudes of the male characters he portrays in his movies: "I think, for all of us, making this movie was like when you get drunk and spurt out your deepest feelings and then the next day you have drunk remorse about what you said. We all feel very proud and a little embarrassed about what we've revealed about ourselves."

4. Shaunti Feldhahn and Jeff Feldhahn, *For Men Only: A Straightforward Guide to the Inner Lives of Women* (Sisters, OR: Multnomah Books, 2006), 119–120.

5. Stephen Arterburn and Fred Stoeker, *Every Young Man's Battle: Strategies for Victory in the Real World of Sexual Temptation* (Colorado Springs, CO: WaterBrook Press, 2002), 62.

6. Michael Kimmel, *Guyland: The Perilous World Where Boys Become Men* (New York: HarperCollins, 2008), 19.

7. See Jesse Owen, Galena Rhoades, Scott Stanley, and Frank Fincham, "'Hooking Up' Among College Students: Demographic and Psychosocial Correlates. *Archives of Sexual Behavior* 39, no. 3 (2010).

8. See Donna Freitas, *Sex and the Soul: Juggling Sexuality, Spirituality, Romance and Religion on America's College Campuses* (New York: Oxford University Press, 2008), 126–133. Alpha males told me things like that it's hard for them to deal with what they call a "sex-only girl" (unbeknownst to the girl, of course) when she wants to start dating, because "they want you to call back and to call them up and hang out, and it's not just after a party and that sort of thing. Like, *during the day!*"

Chapter Six: The Virginity Excuse and Other Modes for Opting Out of Hookup Culture (Sort of)

1. President Clinton denied, under oath, several times, having "sexual relations" with his aide, Monica Lewinsky, although it later came to light that Lewinsky had *at least* performed fellatio on the president. Semen stains on her dress confirmed they had engaged in sexual activity. Clinton denied the allegations throughout the impeachment trial. In some depositions, the terms "sexual affair" or "sexual relations" were not defined, and Clinton held onto the idea that true sexual intercourse was required for the act to be considered as such. In a later deposition, "sexual relations" were defined as "when the person knowingly engages in or causes contact with the genitalia, anus, groin, breast, inner thigh, or buttocks of any person with an intent to arouse or gratify the sexual

desire of any person." Clinton hid behind the questionable loop-
hole of this language, implying that fellatio was not him *engaging*
in the contact, but rather passively receiving. The debate about
what constitutes sex or sexual relations was plunged into the cultural conversation in large part because of these presidential semantic disagreements. See *The Starr Report: The Official Report
of the Independent Counsel's Investigation of the President* (New
York: Random House, 1998) for more details. Excerpts appear
in Kenneth Starr, "The Starr Report: The Independent Counsel's
445-Page Report Details a Relationship and Its Complicated Aftermath [Excerpts]," *Newsweek*, September 21, 1998, 46.

2. See Caitlin Flanagan's "Are You There God? It's Me, Monica," *The Atlantic*, January/February 2006, www.theatlantic.com/
magazine/archive/2006/01/are-you-there-god-it-apos-s-me
-monica/4511/, accessed April 18, 2011. In her article, Flanagan
discussed the "teenage oral-sex craze" and the hysteria about it
among young girls' parents, teachers, and high-school administrators. It all started around the time when Oprah and Dr. Phil
made statements on their TV shows about a "blow-job epidemic," and when Bill Clinton gave us his semantic loopholes
about how he "did not have sex" with Monica Lewinsky. In a
culture of "everything but," oral sex became considered "not
sex," and maybe "just something to do," wrote Flanagan. She
also cited statistics from a National Center for Health Statistics
report released in September 2005, which stated that a quarter
of fifteen-year-old girls and more than half of seventeen-year-
olds had engaged in oral sex. "Fellatio, which was once a part of

the sexual repertoire only of experienced women, is now commonly performed by very young girls outside of romantic relationships, casually and without any expectation of reciprocation," Flanagan wrote. "Nowadays girls don't consider oral sex in the least exotic—nor do they even consider it to be sex. It's just 'something to do.'" Flanagan also delved into the rumored craze of "rainbow parties," as novelized in Paul Ruditis, *Rainbow Party* (New York: Simon Pulse, 2005). In the book—and in the trend—young teenagers have sex parties in which each girl wears a different colored lipstick, and the boys' goal is to end up with a "rainbow" achieved by receiving oral sex from as many girls as possible, and thus collecting as many colors as possible. The book itself—which Flanagan said "mirror[ed] the way girls are said to feel about fellatio: jaded and shockproof"—is only about the planning of such a party, which never comes to fruition. But what it did achieve—among some controversy that perhaps rainbow parties were an urban legend—was at least calling attention to the potentially shocking and bored sex lives of middle-school and high-school students.

3. See Melina M. Bersamin, Deborah A. Fisher, Samantha Walker, Douglas L. Hill, and Joel W. Grube, "Defining Virginity and Abstinence: Adolescents' Interpretations of Sexual Behaviors," *Journal of Adolescent Health* 41, no. 2 (2007): 182–188; Jeremy Uecker, Nicole Angotti, and Mark Regnerus, "Going Most of the Way: 'Technical Virginity' Among American Adolescents," *Social Science Research* 37, no. 4 (2008): 1200–1215; Laura Duberstein Lindberg, Rachel Jones, and John Santelli, "Noncoital Activities

Among Adolescents," *Journal of Adolescent Health* 43, no. 3 (2008): 231–238.

4. Part of this story, as well as discussion of Gabriel's spiritual identity and how it relates to his attitude about sex, appears in my book *Sex and the Soul: Juggling Sexuality, Spirituality, Romance and Religion on America's College Campuses* (New York: Oxford University Press, 2008), 105–106.

5. For the stories of the evangelical students who spoke about the high stakes of purity culture, please see Freitas, *Sex and the Soul*, 75–92, 113–125, and 167–193.

6. In *The Purity Myth: How America's Obsession with Virginity Is Hurting Young Women* (Berkeley, CA: Seal Press, 2010), Jessica Valenti argued that "the lie of virginity—the idea that such a thing even exists—is ensuring that young women's perception of themselves is inextricable from their bodies, and that their ability to be moral actors is absolutely dependent on their sexuality. It's time to teach our daughters that their ability to be good people depends on their *being good people*, not on whether or not they're sexually active" (p. 9). See also Hanne Blank, *Virgin: The Untouched History* (New York: Bloomsbury USA, 2007), for a similar argument and for an examination of historical constructs of virginity, which are, according to the author, almost always female and almost always heterosexual.

7. I also talk about Jamie in *Sex and the Soul*, 100–101.

8. In fact, Jamie was the only person in the entire study to use the words "making love" to refer to sex.

Chapter Seven: Opting Out: Rethinking Abstinence in the Age of Hookup Culture

1. Mark Regnerus, Richard Ross, and Donna Freitas, "The Village Green: What's the Best Way to Encourage People to Save Sex for the Covenant of Marriage?" *Christianity Today*, January 2010, 60–61.

2. Mark Regnerus, *Forbidden Fruit: Sex and Religion in the Lives of American Teenagers* (New York: Oxford University Press, 2007). For more information on Ross's program, see True Love Waits, www.lifeway.com/tlw/, accessed May 2, 2011. When I told the editor that I couldn't answer the question without also explaining why I didn't like the question itself, the editor was still eager to have my opinion included.

3. Regnerus et al., "The Village Green."

4. See, for example, Janet Rosenbaum, "Patient Teenagers? A Comparison of the Sexual Behavior of Virginity Pledgers and Matched Nonpledgers," *Pediatrics* 123, no. 1 (2009): 110–120. This study compared 289 young adults who took a virginity pledge in their teens to 645 young adults who had similar stances on religion, birth control, and sex, but who had not taken such a pledge. Rosenbaum found that five years later, 82 percent of the pledge-takers denied ever having taken the pledge, and there were no differences in sexual activity between the two groups. On the other hand, pledge-takers were less likely to use condoms or birth control. Both groups' members lost their virginity at an average age of twenty-one and had about three lifetime partners; they had similar

rates of sexually transmitted diseases (STDs), and more than 50 percent of the individuals in both groups were having premarital sex. Similarly, Hannah Bruckner and Peter Bearman, in "After the Promise: The STD Consequences of Adolescent Virginity Pledges," *Journal of Adolescent Health* 36, no. 4 (2005): 271–278, found that 88 percent of virginity-pledgers did not wait until they were married to have sex for the first time. Virginity pledges did delay the loss of virginity, but they did not decrease the rate of STDs.

5. I interviewed eighteen evangelical students who had taken a virginity pledge like the one from True Love Waits, and some had taken it as early as middle school. But by the time they were in college, many of them had only vague recollections of taking the pledge. It seems that virginity pledges are more important to younger religious students, such as those in high school and middle school, than to college students. It is not realistic to expect students to avidly swear by such pledges through college and all the way until marriage. See Donna Freitas, *Sex and the Soul: Juggling Sexuality, Spirituality, Romance and Religion on America's College Campuses* (New York: Oxford University Press, 2008), 85.

6. "About the Anscombe Society," blogs.princeton.edu/anscombe/about.html, accessed April 29, 2011.

7. See Iver Peterson, "A Group at Princeton Where 'No' Means 'Entirely No,'" *New York Times*, April 18, 2005.

8. "Abstinence Comes to the Ivy League?" MSNBC.com, last modified October 13, 2005, http://msnbc.msn.com/id/9684205/; "Girls Gone Mild," *Philadelphia Daily News*, October 19, 2005;

Laura Crimaldi, "Princeton Virgins Don't Take Sex-Education Club Lying Down," *Boston Herald*, October 2, 2005.

9. See "MIT Anscombe Society," http://web.mit.edu/anscombe/www/index.shtml, accessed April 29, 2011.

10. "Love & Fidelity Network," http://loveandfidelity.org/default.aspx?ID=7, accessed April 29, 2011.

11. See "The Anscombe Society at Providence College," pcanscombesociety.blogspot.com, accessed April 29, 2011.

12. All quotations in this paragraph were taken from the above-mentioned draft of the proposal for the Center for Abstinence and Chastity. For more information, see "Why Princeton Needs an Abstinence Center," blogs.princeton.edu/anscombe/center-arguments-and-objections.html, accessed April 29, 2011.

13. Jason Sheltzer's column, "Gays, Feminists, and the Anscombe Society," *Daily Princetonian*, December 12, 2007.

14. President Shirley Tilghman's letter to Anscombe rightly highlighted why the society's attitudes about the LGBT community were problematic. She pointed out that discrimination against women and against gay, lesbian, bisexual and transgendered students had often been "stigmatizing, marginalizing and alienating" and that such discrimination had sometimes been "enshrined in law." "In other words," she wrote, discrimination had been "able to draw upon the full force of the state." Furthermore, "LGBT individuals and women are denied fundamental civil rights in many countries around the world, and even in some states within the U.S.A. The same cannot be said for chaste students, which makes the analogy inappropriate, to my way of thinking." But she also wrote,

dismissively, in my opinion: "You argue for such a center on the grounds that abstinent students feel 'stigmatized, marginalized and alienated' when they publicly reject the dominant 'hook-up culture' of the campus. I understand that it is sometimes difficult to stand up for what you believe when you are in the minority, but the fact that you are greeted with opposing points of view when you do so is not sufficient grounds for the University to establish a center." Tilghman's implications about the situation of "chaste students" betrayed exactly the kind of widespread bias about choosing abstinence that the students were complaining about. The social expectation among students and often among faculty, staff, and administrators as well is that it is "normal" for college students to have casual attitudes about sex, that it is "normal" for students to be having a lot of sex at college, that only rarely would a student dissent from this norm, and apparently that dissent exclusively looks like the typical student who joins Anscombe.

15. Among the evangelical students I talked to, "abstinence" and "chastity" had a range of meanings, from avoiding sexual contact besides kissing, to kissing while only standing up, abstaining from kissing in public places, or abstaining from kissing until the engagement or even until the wedding night. Many of the evangelical students hoped to "give their first kiss away" to their future spouse, and most were in agreement about actively avoiding all lustful thoughts until they were married. See Freitas, *Sex and the Soul*, 84–85.

16. The skeptics among scholars, the public, and politicians fuss over the question of whether abstinence education works. A

government-issued report in 2007 showed that abstinence-only education does not work, as students who take part in such programs are just as likely to have sex as everyone else. John Jemmott III, Loretta Jemmott, and Geoffrey Fong, "Efficacy of a Theory-Based Abstinence-Only Intervention over 24 Months: A Randomized Controlled Trial with Young Adolescents," *Archives of Pediatric Adolescent Medicine* 164, no. 2 (2010): 152–159, showed that abstinence-only education *may* reduce the number of students who become sexually active at an early age. Yet this study also had many critics, since the education program encouraged students to delay sex until they were *ready*, not until they were married. See also Rob Stein, "Abstinence-Only Programs Might Work, Study Says," *Washington Post*, February 2, 2010. For further discussion on the debate, see Gail Collins, "The New Anti-Abortion Math," *New York Times*, April 20, 2011, and Roni Caryn Rabin, "New Spending for a Wider Range of Sex Education," *New York Times*, May 10, 2010.

17. See Freitas, *Sex and the Soul*, 156–164, which includes data on peer influence on a student's personal valuing (or devaluing) of sex, having sex, and virginity.

18. Freitas, *Sex and the Soul*, 152.

Chapter Eight: Opting Out of Hookup Culture via The Date

1. Donna Freitas, *Sex and the Soul: Juggling Sexuality, Spirituality, Romance and Religion on America's College Campuses* (New York: Oxford University Press, 2008), 106–109.

2. See, for example, Maria Falzone, Maria Falzone's Sex Rules!, accessed April 3, 2011, www.mariafalzone.com. In addition to stretching a condom over a young man's face, to the audience's great delight, when she lectures, Falzone advises the students about "knowing themselves" with respect to what they want from sex. She goes to great lengths to be inclusive to LGBTQ students. All of this adds up overall to a well-presented, very sex-positive message. Yet, this doesn't quite help students navigate a dating scene, or help to establish one to begin with. There are many other first-year sex-education programs like Falzone's. "Sex Signals," a two-person play that deals with dating and sexual assault, is one of the most popular go-to programs for orientation. Individual speakers, including River Huston and Dr. Sari Locker, have busy fall schedules, too. See Sex Signals, http://bass-schuler.com/sexsignals.php4 and http://www.catharsisproductions.com/sexsignals03.html; also River Huston, www.riverhuston.com/, and Dr. Sari Locker, www.drsari.com/speaking/.

3. Freitas, *Sex and the Soul*, 5.

4. A 2009 study by the Centers for Disease Control and Prevention (CDC) showed that the prevalence of STIs was on the rise in the United States, especially among minorities and young people. Cases of syphilis went up by 5 percent between 2008 and 2009 and by 59 percent from 2005 to 2009. Chlamydia diagnoses rose almost 3 percent from 2008 to 2009; between 2005 and 2009, the CDC reported, "the chlamydia rate in men increased 37.6%, compared with a 20.3% increase in women during this period." See Centers for Disease Control and Prevention,

"National Overview of Sexually Transmitted Diseases (STDs), 2009," in 2009 Sexually Transmitted Disease Surveillance, www.cdc.gov/std/stats09/natoverview.htm, accessed November 2, 2012. See also David Paton and Sourafel Girma, "The Impact of Emergency Birth Control on Teen Pregnancy and STIs," *Journal of Health Economics 30*, no. 2 (2011): 373–380. Paton and Girma's findings showed that a 5 percent increase in STIs among teenagers, and a 12 percent increase in teens under the age of sixteen, were linked to the morning-after pill, likely because of a lower incidence of condom usage.

5. I got the information about Cronin's dating assignment from her firsthand, but several of her tenets for this particular assignment, as well as points she makes in the talks she gives on campus, can be found in Andy Rota, "Cronin Discusses Hooking-Up and Dating," *The Observer at Boston College*, December 12, 2009.

6. Hanna Rosin, "Boys on the Side," *The Atlantic*, September 2012, www.theatlantic.com/magazine/archive/2012/09/boys-on-the-side/309062/, accessed August 24, 2012.

Conclusion: A New Kind of Sex Education: Good Sex 101 and Critical Living Skills

1. Frank Bruni, "The Bleaker Sex," *New York Times*, April 1, 2012, www.nytimes.com/2012/04/01/opinion/sunday/bruni-the-bleaker-sex.html, accessed 4/16/2012.